GENERAL INSTRUCTIONS
(Continued from Page 3)

This will help when painting the individual hairs, which must be transferred and stroked in the proper direction. To transfer the pattern, place the tracing on the painting surface, and slip the transfer paper (coated side down) between your painting surface and tracing paper. (Use gray graphite paper for light surfaces, white Saral for dark surfaces.) Using the ballpoint pen, start transferring the pattern by *lightly* retracing the pattern lines. Slightly lift one corner of your paper to make sure your pattern is transferring correctly, and then proceed. Be careful to transfer all pattern lines accurately and neatly. This is especially important when transferring animal patterns, where hair direction and facial features must be painted accurately for a natural look. (Project instructions will remind you to leave pattern lines exposed when basing in various areas of the designs.)

FINISHING

When you have finished painting the design, allow several days for it to dry and then apply a thin coat of Liquin to the design area. It is important that you cover the entire painting surface; otherwise, there will be shiny spots where areas were glazed. In a few months, when the paint has completely cured, you may want to apply a final protective coating of varnish to your painted piece. For canvas surfaces, use an artist's oil varnish (such as Winsor & Newton Artist's Gloss Varnish); for your wood pieces, use a good-quality semi-gloss varnish.

A FEW SUGGESTIONS BEFORE PAINTING

BRUSH CARE: Before you begin to paint, it is a good idea to dip your brushes into thinner (odorless turpentine) to remove any sizing left in them. Make sure you always wipe excess thinner out of your brushes before loading with paint (a practice that becomes natural after a while); otherwise, your painting surface will become too wet and the paint will run. I wipe my brushes on soft absorbent paper toweling; some people prefer cloth rags. After each painting session, clean paint from brushes with odorless turpentine and blot thoroughly on paper toweling. Rub a bit of baby oil into the hairs and reshape them to their original form. Be sure to stand your brushes upright (bristles/hair pointing upward) when not in use. These practices will help to preserve your brushes.

LAYING OUT YOUR PAINTS: Because these techniques require very little paint, you need only put small amounts on the palette, and add to them as necessary.

PREPARING THE BRUSH: I always carry a bit of Liquin in my brush—it helps to move the paint into the brush hairs when loading and improves the flow during application. Before loading the brush, stroke through a small amount of Liquin until all the hairs are just damp.

CREATING DEPTH IN YOUR PAINTING: It is important to paint trees, bushes and clouds different shapes and sizes, and never in a straight line. If everything is the same size, shape and color, your painting will lack depth.

START SMALL: When painting objects such as rocks, trees, bushes, or clouds, start by creating small shapes, then gradually make the subjects larger. You can always make things bigger, but once the paint is on, it is hard to make things smaller without removing all the paint.

RELAX AND ENJOY: You *can* be a great painter! Try not to become frustrated with your work—it takes time and patience to create a painting. If you get tired of the project, set it aside for another day; chances are it will look better after you have rested. Be proud of what you paint. And remember, painting should be fun! You will never succeed if you never try.

General Terms and Techniques

BASE IN OR BLOCK IN

To "base" or "base in" is to apply the first layer of color to a specific area or object in a design. When two or more base colors are applied side by side, it is sometimes referred to as "blocking in." When colors are blocked in, it is generally necessary to blend the area where the colors meet. (Refer to "Pat Blend.") As you base the design elements, try to paint around pattern lines when possible (this will not be possible where based areas must be blended together). If you lose the lines, it can be very difficult to get features positioned correctly and body parts symmetrically proportioned—a must for a natural look. When a smooth application is desired (eyes and surrounding areas, noses and mouths, for example), use flat sable brushes; for more textured applications (fur, feather areas), I prefer the flat bristle brushes.

BRUSH MIXING

Refer to "Mixing Colors."

DIRTY BRUSH

A dirty brush is one that still carries a bit of paint from the last time it was loaded. When instructed to pick up paint on a dirty brush, do not rinse the paint from the hairs; instead, wipe the brush on paper toweling to remove excess paint, if necessary, before picking up additional color. (Be careful not to overload the brush—only small amounts of paint are required.)

GLAZING

A thin transparent layer of color applied over a dry basecoat is called a "glaze." When applied to large areas, glazes are often referred to as "washes." I use Liquin medium to thin the paint, and flat sable brushes for application. Glazing allows you to see through a layer of paint so the color underneath shows through. I use glazes to add or strengthen shadows and highlights, to tone colors, and to add accent and reflected

(Continued on Page 6)

GENERAL TERMS AND TECHNIQUES
(Continued from Page 5)

colors to skies, rocks, animals, etc. (refer to the color worksheets). For example, when painting the "Wilderness Cascade" landscape, I used purple to deepen the shadows on the rocks, and red and yellow to brighten the sky and give it a glow. I hardly paint anything anymore without glazing something. It is a wonderful technique that just takes a bit of practice.

Before glazing color, make sure the painting surface is completely dry. When glazing larger areas (washing), it is best to apply a thin layer of Liquin to the painting surface, and then lightly stroke thinned paint into it. When glazing smaller areas, use enough Liquin in the brush to thin the color to transparency, and then apply where needed. To ensure that the color is very transparent, load a scant amount of paint on the brush. After loading, always stroke on the palette paper to blend the Liquin medium and paint before applying to painting surface. The nice thing about this technique is that, if it doesn't look right, you can quickly use a clean paper towel to wipe the paint off. Glazing will add depth to your painting and make it come alive. And it's fun to do! Try it!

LAYERING TECHNIQUE

Generally speaking, my basic painting technique can be described as wet-on-wet—meaning I rarely wait for an application to dry completely before adding another layer. However, for me it might be more appropriate to use the term "tacky" rather than "wet." (Refer to "Tack Up.") Because I use Liquin medium (a drying agent) with the fast-drying alkyd paints, applications dry relatively fast and reach the tacky stage quickly. This enables me to apply layer upon layer without waiting for the surface to dry. To apply a color so that it will sit on top of a tacky surface, I use soft brushes (sable or synthetic) and stroke very lightly. If, however, I want the color to blend slightly into a tacky layer (hair strokes, for example), I apply a bit more pressure when stroking. As I wait for an area to tack up, I move on to work in a different area until the previous application is ready for another layer. If a layer of paint has dried beyond the tacky stage before you have finished painting it, Liquin can be applied to allow you to continue to work.

LINEWORK

For fine linework such as tree branches and animal whiskers, paint must be thinned to ink consistency. Thin the paint by dipping the liner into turpentine (leaving most of the turp in the brush) and then stroking it through the paint until the brush is fully loaded. Practice your linework on palette paper first; if the paint is runny and does not produce a line that is consistent in color from start to finish, lightly blot to remove some of the turp from the brush. For lines that are not particularly thin, I sometimes use Liquin on the brush, adding turp only if necessary. Linework is easiest when strokes are pulled toward your body.

LIQUIN MEDIUM

Liquin is a painting medium that is used to speed drying time, improve flow, and thin the consistency of oil and alkyd paints. It is also used as a glazing medium, as well as a final protective coating after the finished painting has dried. As mentioned earlier in this section, I almost always carry a small amount of Liquin in the brush so it will always be damp.

MIXING COLORS

BRUSH MIXING AND LOADING: I prefer to brush mix colors, rather than blending them on the palette with a knife. This way I can get a variety of tones and shades. Because an object or area (animal hair, sky, etc.) is seldom the exact same color throughout, brush mixing will make your painting look more realistic and natural. Before loading, rinse the brush in turpentine and blot on a paper towel. Stroke through Liquin to dampen the hairs. When loading, keep in mind that the painting style for the projects in this book requires very thin layers of color, so it is important to carry only small amounts of paint on the brush, even when brush mixing several colors together. Generally, colors should be picked up one at a time, in the order listed in the instructions. With small amounts of each color on the palette, load the dominant color first, stroking into the paint until the brush is loaded halfway up to the ferule. Move to the next color and pull out a small amount, then gently stroke on the palette to slightly blend the two colors. Continue in this manner until all the colors have been loaded. Be careful not to over blend; you want to be able to see the individual colors on the brush. Rinse the brush in turpentine only when it is necessary to brush mix a new color.

CHANGING THE VALUE: To lighten a color, add Titanium White; to darken, add Ivory Black (or other dark color). Always test a small amount of color by stroking it on the palette before applying it to your painting surface.

USING TITANIUM WHITE:

Warm Titanium White: To **all** your Titanium White, add a touch of Yellow Ochre, Cadmium Yellow Light or Cadmium Orange. This will warm up the white and prevent it from appearing chalky. Although I prefer to brush mix this color as I paint, it might be more convenient to mix it on the palette at the beginning of each painting session. Unless instructed to use Titanium White "straight from the tube," use this warm white mix anytime the instructions call for the use of Titanium White.

Loading Only Titanium White: When instructed to load the brush with Titanium White (not mixed with any other color), rinse all other colors from the brush and load only the warm white mentioned above.

Dirty White: This term refers to white paint that is not "clean" (not pure white), and is usually a created when picking up Titanium White on a brush that still carries color from a previous load. For the projects in this book, this is generally a cool white. If necessary, Dirty White can be mixed by adding a touch of a color such as blue or black to Titanium White.

PAT BLEND

I like to soften all edges so there are no sharp, definite lines. When colors are applied side by side (blocked in), blend the areas where they touch. Blending is done while the paint is wet, lightly patting with clean brushes (unless a "dry" brush is specified, use one that has just a bit of Liquin in it). I generally use bristle brushes where applications need to be less defined or somewhat textured, and sable brushes where a smooth

Supplies

PAINTS

The paints used for the projects in this book are Winsor & Newton Griffin Alkyd Colours. Alkyds are resin-based, fast-drying paints (drying time is about 12 hours) that are compatible with oil-based paints and mediums. Alkyds and oils are often mixed together for the purpose of speeding the drying time of oils. The instructions for the projects in this book are appropriate for both types of paint, so feel free to use whichever you prefer. If you choose to use a different brand of paint, keep in mind that colors may vary in tone and shade from one brand to another, so your colors may not match mine exactly.

On some projects, I have also used black acrylic paint (use your favorite brand); Weber Permalba® Indanthrone Blue oil color; Jo Sonja's® Artists' Colors (acrylic), Brown Earth; and FolkArt® Acrylic Colors, Bluebell. Please check supply lists on individual projects for these colors.

BRUSHES

GRUMBACHER ETERNA WHITE BRISTLE
Series 577F Flat: #6, #10, #20
LOEW-CORNELL LA CORNEILLE® GOLDEN TAKLON
Series 7000 Round: #2
Series 7050 Script Liner: #0
Series 7800 Dagger Striper: 1/8", 3/8"
ROBERT SIMMONS
Series 448 Fan: #2, #4
ROYAL® & LANGNICKEL GOLDEN TAKLON
Series 730 Comb™: 1/4"
ROYAL & LANGNICKEL ROYAL SABLE™
Series 5010 Bright (Flat): #2, #6

GENERAL SUPPLIES

Baby oil (to help preserve your brushes after cleaning)
Jar (for rinsing and cleaning brushes)
Easel, metal or wood (for canvas project)
Gesso, brush-on and spray (optional for preparing surfaces—see "Surface Preparation")
Metal primer (I use Ace Hardware Rust-Stop Gray Primer #16573.)
Odorless turpentine (for cleaning brushes and thinning paint)
Palette, disposable
Palette knife (optional)
Paper towels (the softer and more absorbent, the better)
Pens, fine-point black marker (for tracing patterns) and ball point pen (for transferring design)
Sandpaper, fine-grit
Soft rag or a tack cloth (to remove lint and sawdust)
Sponge brush (for applying sealer and basecoats)
Tracing paper
Transfer paper, gray graphite and Saral (white)
Varnish (artists' oil varnish for canvas, good-quality wood varnish for wood surfaces)
Winsor & Newton Liquin oil painting medium
Wood filler
Wood sealer (I use Ace Hardware Water-Based Sanding Sealer #16063, but you may use the product of your choice.)
Wood stain (I used Ace Hardware Wood Stain, Golden Oak.)

Please check individual projects for special supplies.

Sources

Michaels Arts and Crafts
9386 Hwy. 16
Onalaska, WI 54650   PH: (608) 781-6686
Custom framing of the "Four Season Leaves," and various art supplies

Viking Woodcrafts, Inc.
1317 8th St. S.E.
Waseca, MN 56093   PH: (800) 328-0116
www.vikingwoodcrafts.com
All wood pieces and various art supplies, including Winsor & Newton Griffin Alkyd Colours

General Instructions

SURFACE PREPARATION

WOOD: Repair imperfections with wood filler, if necessary, and allow to dry. Sand surfaces until smooth, and remove all dust with a soft rag or tack cloth. When painting on the raw wood, I recommend sealing the surface before basecoating or staining. There are many good sealers on the market; I use one coat of Ace Hardware Water-based Sanding Sealer #16063, which dries to the touch within 30 minutes. Apply the sealer with a sponge brush; then when dry, sand lightly with fine-grit sandpaper and wipe to remove dust. Next, you can basecoat your surface with white gesso (I use Delta Ceramcoat Artist Gesso, brush-on) or acrylic paint, stain it or leave the natural color showing—whichever you prefer. Be sure to allow each layer of gesso or paint to dry, then sand lightly and remove dust. Transfer the pattern.

METAL: Before painting metal objects (such as milk cans and saw blades), you first need to remove any rust. I prefer taking my item to a sandblaster, but fine-grit sandpaper can be used instead. After sanding, wipe surface to remove dust and dirt. To prevent rust from reappearing, spray with a metal primer and allow to dry. Cover surface with white spray-type gesso (two coats, if necessary), and let this dry completely. This step helps to prepare the surface so it will be smooth. Transfer your pattern.

TRANSFERRING PATTERNS

Use a fine-point black marker pen to trace the pattern onto tracing paper, making sure you include all the detail lines. As you trace the animal patterns, trace the fur lines very carefully.

(Continued on Page 5)

4

PINE TREES
Vary the height

"ALONE" GREY WOLF

FOLIAGE
Paint in clusters, leaving
some dark showing.

LEAVES

BIRCH TREES   BRANCHES
Base in   Shadow   Highlight

FOUR SEASONS
SPRING SCENE

WILDERNESS CASCADE
Use heavier paint when
painting waterfalls.

WINTER SCENE
Wood Box

Halvorson © 2001

effect is desired (noses and eyes, for example). If I have applied color using only one corner of the brush, I often use the clean corner for blending.

REFLECTED COLOR

Sometimes objects can reflect surrounding colors: for example, snow or water may reflect sky colors; animal fur may reflect background colors. Generally these are cool colors—usually blues or grays. Paintings are much more interesting when reflected colors are used to accent specific areas.

SCUFFING

To "scuff" paint onto an area, pick up a small amount of paint on a clean bristle brush (may be dry or slightly dampened with Liquin) and stroke onto a completely dry surface. If there is an underlying base color, I like to leave some of that color showing through the scuffed application.

SHADING AND HIGHLIGHTING

I use several techniques to shade and highlight. In most cases, I allow the base color to tack up, and then lightly stroke shading and highlight colors on top of or into it. When blocking in areas, I often apply highlight or shading color alongside the middle-value color and then blend the area (while wet) where they meet. When I want to avoid having the shading or highlight color blend with the base color (highlights on the black cow in the "Kissin' Cowsins" project, for example), I allow the surface to dry completely and then scuff or glaze the area. (Refer to "Scuffing" and "Glazing.")

TACK UP

This term describes the texture of paint when it has begun to dry and becomes somewhat "set." When paint has reached the "tacky" stage, it will still be wet enough to allow another color to be lightly blended into it, yet set enough that it will not lift from the surface during the process. If an area has dried beyond the tacky stage before you have finished painting it, use a sable brush to lightly stroke a thin layer of Liquin over the area, and then continue painting. While you wait for paint to tack up in one area, move on to work another area when possible.

Developing Fur

When I first started painting, my love was landscapes and florals. Often I would say, "I will never paint animals." Now animals are among my very favorite subjects to paint. It also helps that my husband and I are both dedicated and devoted animal lovers.

Because of my love of animals, I would like to dedicate the animal projects in this book to a very special friend, whose name is Duke. Four years ago, my father passed on and we inherited his faithful companion—the cutest Chinese pug you ever did see. We didn't realize then that, through such a difficult time, this little dog would bring so much joy into our lives. Duke eats with us, plays with us, and Duke *does* sleep with us. Presently, Duke is experiencing heart failure, but we know that every day we have had him has been a blessing.

When painting animals, you will need to work your fur over and over again, applying many layers until you are satisfied with the look. Although this technique is time consuming, the end results are very rewarding. The "Bear Cabinet" project is an excellent example of this process, where I applied layer upon layer of hair, highlights, shadows, markings and reflected color. This cannot be accomplished in a single painting session!

For a realistic painting, it is important to paint animal fur in the direction you would pet the animal, or the direction it naturally grows. It will help to follow your pattern lines as accurately as possible when applying the individual hair strokes. Make sure you work in groupings or clusters—you do not want to see individual hairs that are all the same length or lined up in a row. It is especially important that you always (and often!) refer to the color photos and worksheets as you paint.

You will notice in the project instructions that the eyes and the surrounding area are painted before you begin to develop the fur. Please refer to individual projects for those instructions.

BASING LIGHT AND DARK AREAS

After painting the eye areas, base in the general light and dark areas of the head and body according to the individual project instructions. Blend the areas where the colors meet. (Refer to "Pat Blend.") Remember to leave the main patterns lines showing, where possible (facial features, shape of head, ears and limbs). These lines will be covered with layers of hair later.

LAYERING INDIVIDUAL HAIR STROKES

On the color worksheet, notice the different ways to paint fur. Although I have illustrated how to use a variety of brushes to paint the different types of fur, it is difficult to teach without being right there with you. Before actually painting the project, it is best to practice on palette paper. Taking classes can also be a very big help. Listed below are the brushes I use, along with instructions on how I use them. Please feel free to use the brushes you are most comfortable with.

DAGGER BRUSH: Depending upon the type of animal being painted and the length and type of fur, I sometimes use a variety of brushes. However, the brush I most often use (almost always, actually) for painting individual hairs is the Loew-Cornell 7800 Dagger Striper, sizes 1/4" and 3/8". (Notice the unique shape of the brush and different lengths of the hairs.) I use the smaller size for shorter hair, and the larger size for longer hair. Before loading with paint, always rinse the brush in turpentine to remove any sizing in the hairs. Thin the paint to ink consistency using Winsor & Newton Liquin

(Continued on Page 8)

DEVELOPING FUR

(Continued from Page 7)

medium. To do so, stroke the brush through Liquin until all the hairs are coated, and then stroke through paint. Stroke the brush on the palette until paint and medium are evenly distributed throughout the hairs. If the Liquin does not make the paint thin enough to pull a smooth, thin stroke, add a bit of turpentine to the brush. To apply the paint, hold the brush almost straight up and down and use very light pressure as you stroke. If you are using it correctly, the brush will be somewhat fanned out as you stroke, making it possible to apply several individual hairs at once. (This *does* take some practice!)

FAN BRUSH: For very long fur on a large project, I sometimes use a fan brush. There is an example of long fur on the color worksheet, which was taken from the wolf in the "Alone Wolf" project. I thin my paint slightly by dipping the bristles into turpentine, lightly blotting on paper towel and then stroking through the paint. Instead of painting from the flat side of the brush, I tip the brush on its side and use the lower corner of the chisel edge to pull the strokes. I repeat these steps over and over again.

LINER BRUSH: On the color worksheet there is an illustration of a wolf's ear, taken from the "Resting Wolf" project. Notice that the hairs inside the ears are relatively long and fine. These hairs were painted with a #0 script liner brush, and the paint was thinned with turpentine to ink consistency. (Refer to "Linework.") Again, pay attention to the direction of the individual hairs. The liner brush also works well for shorter hairs toward the front of the face.

COMB BRUSH: I use the comb brush when I want to paint clusters of individual hairs (top of the head and edges of skin folds on "Resting Wolf project). To thin the paint, stroke the brush through Liquin and then through the paint. Make some practice strokes on the palette paper; if the strokes are not thin enough, add a bit of turp to the brush.

Before painting the first layer of hair, allow the paint in the based areas to tack up. When painting the first layers, use colors that contrast with the based areas (light over dark; dark over light). Allow the base colors to show through the individual hairs to define where there are dark markings and shadowed folds in the skin. As you add more layers, use colors and values that show the full range of the natural fur coloration.

Begin by painting the hair around the eye areas, and then progress toward the back of the animal. Pull the hair strokes slightly beyond the outer edges of each area (this will cover any exposed pattern lines). When you have completed the first layer, allow the paint to tack up and apply another layer. If the paint becomes too dry to move as you stroke additional layers, apply a thin layer of Liquin to the area you are working and then continue painting. (Be sure to stroke very lightly when applying the Liquin so the underlying layer of paint will not lift from the surface.) Continue layering hair until you are satisfied with the overall look. Use the tip of the liner brush to paint the dots at the base of the whiskers and to then paint the whiskers. Using a flat or bristle brush (your choice), soften and fade all the edges where the fur meets the background areas.

GLAZING AND FINAL DETAIL

When you are satisfied with the painting and feel that it is complete, allow it to dry thoroughly. Study your painting to decide whether you need to add more hair or color (shadows, highlights, markings, reflected color). If necessary, apply glazes to make adjustments. Be sure to first review "Glazing" in the front of the book. Working in one area at a time, follow the glazing instructions to apply transparent color where needed. *NOTE: Do not attempt to reach the desired strength of color with one heavy application to each area. Remember that these glazes must be very transparent to achieve a realistic look, so you may need to repeat this process many times before the color in these areas is strong enough.* During the glazing process, continue to add layers of individual hairs to give more depth and density to the fur.

Bear Cabinet
Color Photo on Front Cover

This bear was photographed at Como Park Zoo in St. Paul, Minnesota. Although I chose to paint on wood, the same instructions would apply for painting on canvas. Out of all the projects in this book, this and "'Alone' Grey Wolf" were the most time consuming, but they were also the ones I was most pleased with. Whatever you do, keep at it—don't give up! Take your time; it will be worth it in the end!

PALETTE
WINSOR & NEWTON GRIFFIN ALKYD COLOURS
Alizarin Crimson
Burnt Sienna
Burnt Umber
Cadmium Orange
Cadmium Red Light
Cadmium Yellow Light
Ivory Black
Sap Green
Titanium White
Yellow Ochre
WEBER PERMALBA OIL COLORS
Indanthrone Blue

MEDIUM BLUE MIX: Indanthrone Blue + a touch of Burnt Sienna + enough Titanium White to produce a medium gray-blue

BRUSHES
Comb: 1/4"
Dagger: 1/8", 3/8"
Flat Bristle: #10, #20
Flat Sable: #2, #6
Round: #2
Script liner: #0

SPECIAL SUPPLIES
Black acrylic paint
FolkArt Acrylic Colors, Bluebell (#909)
Real maple leaves (optional)
Soft, lint-free cloth
Wood stain (I used Ace Hardware Wood Stain, Golden Oak.)

PREPARATION
Remove the door panel. Prepare the wood following directions under "Surface Preparation" in the "General Instructions" section of the book. Apply two coats of black acrylic paint to the panel and allow it to dry. Transfer the pattern for the bear.

I stained the cabinet with Golden Oak wood stain. The trim was painted with a sponge brush and Bluebell acrylic paint. When dry, I antiqued the blue trim by dulling the color with a wash of Burnt Umber and Liquin. Rub this on with a soft rag, then wipe off excess.

PAINTING INSTRUCTIONS
Before you start the bear, study the color worksheet and photo, and refer to them often.

BACKGROUND
Load a #10 flat bristle brush with Indanthrone Blue, and then tone it down with a touch of Burnt Sienna—this color should be very dark. Using overlapping "x" strokes, apply color to the background area around the right side of the bear's body and below the arms. With the background color still in the brush, pick up a touch of Titanium White (this is the Medium Blue Mix). Using "x" strokes, apply a touch of this color to the upper right corner of the panel, and then soften the edges into the background.

BEAR
EYES, NOSE AND MOUTH: These eyes are very similar to the "Resting Wolf" project. Please refer to those instructions to paint the eyeballs and the area around each eye. Base the nose, mouth and chin with Ivory Black (detail will be painted later). Using the #0 liner and Medium Blue Mix, add the highlight line underneath each eye and paint a dash for the sparkle at the top of each eye. Use the tip of the liner brush and Titanium White to add the sparkle dot on top of the dash. After the eye areas have dried completely, use a #2 flat sable and Burnt Umber to glaze across the upper corners of the eyes, to give them a touch more depth. Make sure you keep this out of the sparkle.

BODY AND HEAD: Using enough Liquin on the #10 flat bristle brush to thin the paint, base the entire body and head with Burnt Umber + a touch of Burnt Sienna. Remember to stroke in the direction the hair naturally grows. Try to leave the pattern lines slightly exposed. When you get to the dark area between the chin and paws, add Ivory Black to the base color on the brush. To paint around the claws, use the same dark color but switch to a #2 flat sable brush.

LAYERING INDIVIDUAL HAIRS (Body and Head): Begin by very carefully reading "Developing Fur" at the front of the book. Refer to the color photo to see where colors are placed. On palette paper, practice using the dagger and comb brushes, making clusters and individual hair strokes (use any of the dark colors listed below). Remember that the paint has to be thin or the bristles will not fan out correctly. Once you learn to use these brushes correctly, you will be fascinated by what you can do with them.

Paint the individual hairs on the head and back (shoulders and arms will be painted later), using brush mixes of Titanium White + each of the following colors: Burnt Umber, Burnt Sienna and Yellow Ochre. After each layer, allow the surface to tack up before applying the next. Use the Medium Blue Mix for the reflected color on the head (ears, forehead, around eyes, under chin, top of head) and body (top edge of neck fold and upper edge of back, left side). Notice that there are patches of lighter hairs on the top of the head and ears, and lighter markings around the eyes and nose; use the Yellow Ochre + Titanium White mix for these areas. To define sharper edges where individual hairs are very short (the narrow section of muzzle, to the right of the nose, for example), switch to a #6

(Continued on Page 11)

Bear Cabinet

BEAR CABINET
(Continued from Page 9)

flat sable brush and use the chisel edge to apply color. When each layer of hair has been completed, soften the bases (root ends) with a slightly damp comb brush. This will set them in. Reinforce the dark shadows on the face with hair strokes of Burnt Umber and Burnt Sienna. Rework the fur, as many times as necessary, until you are satisfied that it is dense enough. Remember to soften the hair around the outer edges into the background.

DETAIL ON NOSE AND MOUTH AREA: With a #2 flat sable brush, first highlight the nose with a dash of Medium Blue Mix, and then use Titanium White for the extra shine in the center of the dash. Gently pat the edges of both highlight applications to soften slightly, then wipe the brush on a paper towel. Load one flat side of the dirty brush with Ivory Black + a touch of Titanium White to produce a dirty-looking gray, and then paint the teeth, pulling very short, downward strokes. With the #2 round brush, highlight the teeth with some of the gray color + a bit of Titanium White. If you want more of a division between the teeth, pull a bit of Ivory Black between a couple of them. To soften the color in the teeth area, pat blend with a clean #6 sable brush. Use the round brush and Ivory Black to shade just under the teeth. Using lighter colors, add detail hair under the mouth.

LAYERING INDIVIDUAL HAIRS (Shoulders and Arms): Use the comb and the dagger to start shaping these areas. Pay close attention to the direction and flow of the hair. Use all the same colors as before, but mix darker values this time. Use the Medium Blue Mix for reflected color on the right shoulder— this will put this area in the shadows. With a dry #20 flat bristle brush, pat blend to soften the fur of the shoulders and arm areas and to fade the edges into the background.

CLAWS: Base the claws with the #2 flat sable brush, using the same gray mix used to base the teeth. Wipe the brush, pick up Ivory Black, and then shade the claws. Use the Medium Blue Mix to add reflected color. Wash the brush in turpentine and blot well on paper towel. Pick up Titanium White (not thinned) and add highlights. Using a dry #6 flat sable and stroking vertically, lightly slim the surface to soften all the colors. This last step will help shape the claws and make them appear rounded.

LEAVES

I gathered real leaves to use as patterns, but you may prefer to use the pattern provided. Let the entire painting dry completely before painting the leaves. Use all the colors used for the bear plus touches of Sap Green, Cadmium Orange and Cadmium Red Light. The brightest colors in the leaves are Yellow Ochre and Cadmium Yellow Light mixed individually with Titanium White. When painting leaves, always pull the strokes toward the center vein. Base the leaves by blocking in the various colors with the #6 flat sable brush, and then blend where the colors meet. Use the same brush and a variety of light colors to highlight the edges. Add accents with Medium Blue Mix. Pull vein lines on each leaf with the #0 liner and thinned paint, using a color that is darker than the leaf itself.

GLAZING AND FINAL DETAIL

When the entire painting has tacked up, study your work and decide whether you want to repeat some of the steps above to add more shadows, highlights and hair to the bear. When you have finished these steps and have allowed the painting to dry completely, glaze the background area along the edge of the bear, using Indanthrone Blue + Ivory Black. This will bring out the colors in the bear and give the background depth. To add depth to the leaves, use glazes to strengthen some of the darker base colors on a few, then use Ivory Black + a touch of Alizarin Crimson to add shading here and there. Use various shades of Ivory Black + Alizarin Crimson to paint shadows behind some of the leaves. When glazing, remember to use very small amounts of paint and enough Liquin in the brush to produce transparent color. Take your time with this piece. Sign your name, you are finished!

FINISHING

Allow the painting to dry, then apply a thin coat of Liquin to the design area. Varnish the rest of the piece with a wood varnish of your choice. When the painting has cured, varnish the design area if you wish.

Eagle

Color Photo on Front Cover

Living in Minnesota, I have had the opportunity to view many majestic eagles soaring over our beautiful lakes. There is just something spiritual, serene and patriotic about this beautiful bird. Although I chose to paint on a wood piece, feel free to paint on a surface of your choice.

PALETTE

WINSOR & NEWTON GRIFFIN ALKYD COLOURS
Burnt Sienna
Burnt Umber
Cadmium Orange
Cadmium Yellow Light
Cerulean Blue Hue
Ivory Black
Titanium White
Yellow Ochre
WEBER PERMALBA OIL COLORS
Indanthrone Blue

BRUSHES

Dagger: 1/8" (optional)
Flat bristle: #10
Flat sable: #2, #6
Round: #2
Script liner: #0

SPECIAL SUPPLIES

Jo Sonja's Artists' Colors, Brown Earth (acrylic)
Wood stain (I used golden oak.)

PREPARATION

Follow the instructions under "Surface Preparation" in the "General Instructions" section of the book. Paint the entire inside of the tray with Jo Sonja's Brown Earth. When dry, apply a second coat and let that dry. Sand lightly and wipe sanding dust. Transfer the pattern with white transfer paper. Stain the outside and rim of the tray with the color of your choice.

PAINTING INSTRUCTIONS

BACKGROUND

Before you begin, study the color photo to see where the background changes in color and value. Apply the background colors with the #10 flat bristle brush, using loose "x" strokes. Start in the lower left corner of the tray with Burnt Umber, Indanthrone Blue and a touch of Burnt Sienna on the brush, and work clockwise around the eagle. As you work toward the center, where the color is more blue than brown, wipe the brush on a paper towel and gradually start picking up Cerulean Blue Hue and a touch of Burnt Sienna, adding Titanium White as necessary to lighten the mix. You will notice in the photo that the lightest area is next to the left side of the eagle. When you reach the area above the forehead, pick up Indanthrone Blue and Burnt Sienna. Continue picking up these colors until you approach the area toward the back of the neck, then add Burnt Umber to the blue on the brush to make this area almost black. With a dry flat bristle brush, lightly blend the light and dark areas together, but not so much that you blur out all of the

"x" strokes—you want the effect to be mottled. Using the darkest background mix, paint the inner surfaces of the sides of the tray (the sides will be glazed later).

EAGLE

EYE AND SURROUNDING AREA: (Refer to the color worksheet illustration and study the close-up of the eagle eye carefully.) Using a #2 flat sable brush and very little paint, paint the lower half of the iris with Cadmium Yellow Light, the sides with Cadmium Orange, then add Burnt Sienna to each corner. Pat blend to soften between each color with a #2 flat sable brush. Fill in the pupil and area just around the eye with Ivory Black. Scuff around the black area around the eye with a dry flat brush, using Burnt Umber, then Burnt Sienna, and then Titanium White, allowing some of the Brown Earth basecoat color to show through. (The top half of the eye will be glazed later.) Notice in the photo that there are two areas, just to the right of the beak and to the left of the eye, that are very dark. Pick up Ivory Black and Burnt Umber on a very dry brush and scuff these areas, making sure your strokes follow the natural contours around the beak and eye. When this last step has been completed, you will have filled in the entire area around the eye with color. To paint the broken highlight line underneath and to the left of the iris, use the #0 liner and Cadmium Orange + just a touch of Titanium White. Pick up any blue that is on the palette and add a bit of Dirty White, then place a small dash where the sparkle will be. Using the liner brush and thinned Titanium White, add the sparkle dot.

BEAK: Using the #6 flat sable brush, block in the colors for the beak, but do not paint over the pattern lines that separate the sections. You will need to refer to the color photo to see where to place the colors. Base the yellow areas with Cadmium Yellow Light and the shaded areas with Burnt Sienna, then blend these colors together where they meet. Allow the paint to tack up, and then strengthen the darkest areas of the shaded areas with Burnt Umber, again softly blending the colors where necessary. Using a clean, flat sable brush and Titanium White, add the brightest highlights to the beak, then soften the edges. Repeat the highlight step if necessary. Paint the nose hole with Burnt Umber, then soften around the edges. When the paint has tacked up, accent each section of the beak with a bit of Cadmium Orange.

HEAD, NECK AND SHOULDER: With the #10 flat bristle brush, base in the head and neck with Titanium White + a touch of Indanthrone Blue (use ample Liquin on the brush for a somewhat thin application). If this color is too bright, add a bit of Burnt Umber to tone it down to a medium blue-gray.

Wash the color from the brush and wipe it dry. Pick up Burnt Umber + a touch of Indanthrone Blue and fill in the shoulder area, leaving a slight separation between the neck and the shoulder.

Now, using the chisel edge of the #6 flat sable brush, go back to the head and start adding individual hair-like feathers with Titanium White. Be careful to pull the strokes in the direction of the pattern lines. As you paint the feathers, make

(Continued on Page 14)

Eagle

EAGLE

(Continued from Page 12)

sure you leave some of the blue base color showing through to serve as shading. I started at the top of the head and worked downward. For the very brightest feathers, add Cadmium Yellow Light to the Titanium White. Toward the very top of the head, "flick" in (quick, upward strokes) some individual hairs with a #0 liner. If you have trouble getting the paint to move easily, add a bit of turpentine to the liner. When you have finished painting the feathers, allow the surface to tack up, then use a flat sable brush to add shading and accent colors. I picked up a blue mix from the palette and stroked this onto the center of the cheek and neck; I added touches of Burnt Sienna and Yellow Ochre to the cheek and front of the neck; and I shaded under the chin with Burnt Umber. Allow the paint to tack up again; then, using Titanium White and the same brushes as before, go back to the whitest areas and add a few more feathers. Using the liner and Titanium White, stroke some thin lines through the darker-colored areas.

Using a #10 flat bristle brush, highlight the shoulder with Burnt Sienna + a touch of Titanium White, then soften the edges.

GLAZING

Allow the painting to dry completely. Glaze shading across the top of the eye with Burnt Umber, and glaze Ivory Black between the neck and shoulder to deepen the shading. Glaze a wash of Ivory Black + Burn Umber over the inner surfaces of the sides of the tray. Using the same mix, glaze sheer color in the darkest area of the background and around the edges of the design area. When you have finished with these last steps, look carefully at your painting and decide whether you want to add additional shadows, highlights, accents and feathers. Do not be afraid to try making some feathers with a dagger brush.

FINISHING

When you are satisfied with the end results, sign your name! Allow the painting to dry. Apply a thin coat of Liquin to the entire design area. When cured, varnish with the product of your choice.

Wilderness Cascade
Color Photo on Front Cover

Last year I had the opportunity to visit Lake Tahoe. Absolutely breathtaking. Some portions of this painting were designed from the photos I took while there; some are from my own imagination. Feel free to paint this on canvas, driftwood, or surface of your choice. When painting bushes, trees and rocks, don't be afraid to use your own creativity. There are no specific forms or numbers for creations of nature, so do your own thing; put in as many trees and rocks as you want. Throughout this painting, it is important to refer to the color worksheet often.

PALETTE
WINSOR & NEWTON GRIFFIN ALKYD COLOURS
Burnt Umber
Cadmium Red Light
Cadmium Yellow Light
Cerulean Blue Hue
Ivory Black
Titanium White
Viridian
WEBER PERMALBA OIL COLORS
Indanthrone Blue

MIXES

Besides the palette colors listed, three basic mixes will be used. If you are more comfortable using a palette knife to mix these colors before you begin to paint, mix a fairly good-sized pile of each color.

BLUE MIX: Mix Indanthrone Blue and a touch of Ivory Black, then mix in Titanium White until you have a toned-down medium blue. I use this mix in the sky, the rocks, water and fog.

DARK GREEN MIX: Mix Indanthrone Blue, a touch of Ivory Black and a small amount of Cadmium Yellow Light. This mix should be a very dark green. I used this mix for the pine trees and dark foliage.

PURPLE MIX: Mix Indanthrone Blue and Cadmium Red Light, then keep adding Titanium White until you have a toned-down medium purple. Too much Cadmium Red Light will make the mix too gray. This mix will be used in the sky, rocks, distant background hills and water.

BRUSHES
Bristle: #10
Fan: #2, #4
Flat sable: #6
Script liner: #0

SPECIAL SUPPLIES
Gesso
Wood stain (I used golden oak.)

PREPARATION

Refer to "Surface Preparation" in the "General Instructions" section of the book. Apply gesso to the lid. Stain the basket with golden oak or color of your choice. Transfer the pattern.

PAINTING INSTRUCTIONS

Please study the color photo and worksheet illustrations carefully before painting this project.

SKY

Before you begin painting, look at the lightest area of the sky (this is mainly the center). Where you see streaks of yellow and orange, leave this area unpainted for now. Paint the sky with horizontal strokes, using the #10 flat bristle brush. Start by applying the Purple Mix in the upper corners of the sky area. Next to this, streak in the Blue Mix and then Titanium White + a touch of Cadmium Red Light. Blend these colors into each other as you apply the paint. Now wash and clean the brush thoroughly. Pick up a small amount of Titanium White and Cadmium Yellow Light and, beginning at the center of the horizon line, apply color, stretching the paint out until it meets the darker colors. Be careful that you don't get the yellow into the Blue Mix area or you will have a green sky. Soften and blend where the colors meet. Load the #4 fan brush with fairly thick Titanium White, and turn the brush over so the paint is on the top side. Now "puff" a couple of cloud shapes into the sky by pushing the edge of the brush against the surface so the paint almost "falls" off the brush. With a dry sable brush, soften these areas into the various colors of the sky, and then blend across the bottoms of the clouds to set them in. After the paint has tacked up a bit, you may want to pull some of the Purple Mix into the outer edges of the sky.

DISTANT HILL AND TREES

Load the corner of the #10 flat bristle brush with the Purple Mix + a touch of Titanium White, and base in the distant hills, stroking up and down. To highlight the hills, I used both the Purple Mix and the Blue Mix, adding more Titanium White to each. Load the corner of the #2 fan brush and turn the brush over so the paint is on the top, then tap in some lighter highlights along the horizon line. Use the sable brush to soften the highlights.

Notice that there is an indication of a few distant pine trees in front of the hills. To paint these, pick up Dark Green Mix on the #2 fan brush, and add Titanium White until it becomes a medium-value green (load only a small amount of paint on the brush), then tap up and down to apply the color. These trees are not formed, nor are they detailed. When you are finished painting the trees, soften the bases using dry #10 flat bristle brush and a gentle circular motion. Clean the paint from the brush and dry it well.

FOG

The distant fog (below the distant trees and above the rocks) is painted with Titanium White + a very small amount of the Purple Mix. Load very little paint on one corner of the flat bristle brush, and start making small circular motions, beginning at the very bottom and working your way upward. As you get to the top of the fog area, you shouldn't have any paint left on the brush. To blur the fog into the trees, very lightly touch the brush to the area where the two meet. Basically, all the fog in the painting will be done this exact same way.

ROCKS

If at any time the during the process of painting the rocks they become muddy and start looking like they are all one color, let the paint tack up and paint over them.

Using a #10 flat bristle brush, base in lighter-colored rocks with the Purple Mix, and the darker rocks with Burnt Umber. Allow the paint to tack up before continuing.

The darker shading colors are various combinations of the Blue and Purple Mixes, lightened when necessary with touches of Titanium White. Using the #6 sable brush, apply these colors to shade the lighter rocks and to establish medium-value color on some of the darker rocks. I accented these areas here and there with a touch of Cerulean Blue Hue. It is such a pretty color.

When adding highlights to the light-colored rocks, use the #6 flat sable brush and load with heavier paint for a more textured application. To reflect some of the sky colors, highlight the lightest rocks with Cadmium Yellow Light + Titanium White, and mix a small amount of Cadmium Red Light, Cadmium Yellow Light and Titanium White to highlight and cast an orange tint on others.

Highlight the tops and sides of some of the darker rocks with Cadmium Red Light + Titanium White. This has a pinkish cast to it. When highlighting the sides, load the brush fully, but use the chisel edge to apply the paint. Place this color where you want it to be lightest and brightest, and then pull the edges into the surrounding colors.

After the paint has tacked up slightly, use a flat sable brush to skim some green tones here and there on the rocks.

WATER AND WATERFALL

Using the Purple Mix and the #10 flat bristle brush, paint the water below the waterfall, pulling the strokes from the top of this area straight down, almost to the bottom of the lid. Base in the area along the bottom edge of the lid with the Blue Mix. Using a clean, dry flat sable brush, very lightly skim back and forth across the surface of the water to blend these colors slightly. (The white water will be painted later.) With a #10 flat bristle and the Blue Mix, base in the waterfall, pulling the color from the top of the fall to the bottom. Allow the paint to tack up. Load a corner of the #2 fan brush with Titanium White, and lightly pull a stroke from the very top to the bottom of each section of the fall. Make sure you follow the curve of the fall, and try not to stop and start these strokes—pull one smooth stroke for each section. If the paint doesn't move smoothly, you may need to pick up additional Liquin on the brush.

To paint the heavier splashes and foam at the bottom of the waterfall, load the corner of the fan brush with Titanium White, and then turn the brush so the paint is on the top. In a manner similar to painting a bush, tap the color into the blue water. Start with the splashes just under the lower fall and move down into the water, tapping until there is no more paint on the brush. Use a dry flat sable brush to pat around the edges of these splashes to soften them out into the calmer water. You may need to repeat these steps a few times, allowing the paint to tack up between applications. On the lower section of the fall, the cascading water is splashing a bit more than the higher sections. Load the fan brush with Titanium White and use chisel edge to tap in this white water as it cascades down the falls.

(Continued on Page 17)

Wilderness Cascade

WILDERNESS CASCADE
(Continued from Page 15)
PINE TREES AND BUSHES

The secret to painting pine trees is to have plenty of paint on the brush. I prefer to use a newer fan brush for pine trees. If you are not comfortable using the fan brush, you could also use a flat bristle brush. It might be helpful to practice these on the palette paper. Pick up the Dark Green Mix on a corner of the #2 fan brush and pull strokes for the trunks; then start putting in the darker, shaded branches, tapping horizontally. For the highlights, simply add a touch of Titanium White to the Dark Green Mix, and tap color into some of the dark branches. Add highlights to both sides of the tree, but place more on the side facing the light source—be careful not to add too many to the light side, or the tree will look like it was cut in half. For a few brighter highlights on the lightest trees, add Cadmium Yellow Light + Titanium White to the very tops.

The bushy foliage around the rocks is based in with the corner of a #2 fan brush, using the same colors as for the pine trees. These mixes need to be a fairly heavy consistency. Hold the brush so the edge is horizontal and tap the paint off the corner, working the foliage into groupings and clusters. Add highlights, again using the same colors that were used in the pine trees. Once in a while, pick up a touch of Viridian with these mixes, just to add some interest. Using the #0 liner brush and any of the green mixes, thinned to ink consistency, pull up some weeds near the front of the design.

REMAINING FOG

When the painting is fairly dry, add the fog around the rocks and pine trees, following the instructions above for the distant fog.

BARE TREES AND BRANCHES

Load the #6 flat sable brush with Burnt Umber + Ivory Black, and use the chisel edge to base the larger trees. Start at the base of the tree and pull upward. Use the #0 liner and thinned paint to paint the smaller trees. Load one side of the flat sable with a touch of Cadmium Red Light + Cadmium Yellow Light mixed with Titanium White. Using the chisel edge of the brush, lay the paint on the very outside edge of the light side of the tree (this applications needs to be a bit heavier than usual). Using a chopping stroke, work a bit of the paint toward the middle of the tree to make it resemble tree bark. To set the trees into the ground, pull up weeds or paint foliage in front of the bases. Or you can set them into the ground by patting the very bottoms to blur them out.

GLAZING

This is another one of those paintings that would be fun to glaze. When the painting is completely dry, try glazing additional sunlight to the sky, using reds and yellows, and perhaps darkening the bases of the rocks with glazes of Ivory Black.

FINISHING

Remember to sign your name! If you applied glazes, allow the surface to dry completely, then apply a couple coats of Liquin to the entire design. Allow the paint to cure, and apply the finishing product of your choice.

Curious Critter Magazine Rack
Color Photo on Page 21

This little critter was photographed at Oxbow Park near Byron, Minnesota, one of my very favorite places to take pictures. Although small in size, Oxbow Park has a wide variety of wildlife. It is truly a unique place to visit.

If you prefer, this project could be painted on a 9" x 12" stretched canvas instead of the magazine rack.

PALETTE
WINSOR & NEWTON GRIFFIN ALKYD COLOURS
Burnt Sienna
Burnt Umber
French Ultramarine
Ivory Black
Sap Green or Viridian (for leaves)
Titanium White
Yellow Ochre

MIXES

Because you will be using these three basic mixes throughout the painting, you may prefer to use a palette knife to mix three piles of paint on your palette paper before you begin to paint. If you should run out, mix again and get as close to the original as you can.

MEDIUM BLUE MIX: Mix equal amounts of French Ultramarine, Ivory Black and Titanium White. This should be a medium blue, not too bright. If the blue becomes too bright, add a touch more of Ivory Black.

MEDIUM BROWN MIX: Mix equal amounts of Burnt Umber and Burnt Sienna, then gradually add Titanium White until you have a nice medium brown color. Do not get this too washed out or allow it to become beige. I would rather have it a bit toward the darker side than too light.

HIGHLIGHT WHITE MIX: Mix equal amounts of Yellow Ochre and Titanium White, then add a touch of Burnt Sienna to make it a slightly golden color.

BRUSHES
Dagger: 1/8"
Flat bristle: #6, #10
Flat sable: #2, #6
Round: #2
Script liner: #0

(Continued on Page 18)

CURIOUS CRITTER MAGAZINE RACK

(Continued from Page 17)

SPECIAL SUPPLIES

Black acrylic paint
Wood stain, golden oak color

PREPARATION

Follow the instructions under "Surface Preparation" in the "General Instructions" section of the book. Basecoat the front panel and the inner edge of the magazine rack with black acrylic paint, using either a flat synthetic or sponge brush, and allow to dry. (Remember to wash the brush with water to clean out the acrylic paint.) Stain all other surfaces with a golden oak stain. When dry, transfer your patterns.

PAINTING INSTRUCTIONS

In the "General Terms and Techniques" section of the book, I suggested that you warm up your white, using either yellow or orange. Usually it does not matter which color you use, but for this particular project, I prefer Yellow Ochre because it complements the wood tones.

RACCOON

BLOCKING IN LIGHT AND DARK AREAS: When basing the raccoon, try not to paint over the pattern lines; they will be covered later as you apply the hair. You do not need heavy coverage for these areas, so use the paint sparingly. You'll want to be able to see some of the basecoat color through the white areas. Base all the dark areas with Ivory Black (this includes everything except the white areas on the muzzle and forehead). Use a #10 flat bristle brush for the top of the head and inside the ears, leaving a quarter-inch space around the outer edge of each ear for the white outline. Use the #2 flat sable for the eyes and mask area around eyes; and use the #6 flat sable for the nose and mouth. When applying the base colors, stroke in the direction that the hairs would naturally be growing. Next, use the #10 flat bristle brush and Titanium White to fill in the white areas of the mask and muzzle. Paint the outer edge of each ear with a slightly heavier coverage of Titanium White, using the #2 flat sable brush.

HAIR AROUND EDGES OF EARS: The very short hairs around the edges of the ears are applied with the 1/8" dagger brush dampened with turpentine (do not load with paint). To stroke these individual hairs, hold the brush so that it is almost vertical, and use the edge with the longer hairs to pull Titanium White from the based edge, "flicking" (short, quick, upward motion) the strokes slightly over the edge of the ear. Although this is a fun step, you must be careful not to make the hairs too long. If you are more comfortable using a liner, just moisten the very tip with turpentine (no paint on the brush) and pull paint out of the white based edge. This method will also work well.

EYES: Using the #0 liner and Medium Blue Mix thinned to ink consistency, outline the eyeballs on both sides, but do not make a full circle. Place a dash of Medium Blue Mix at the top of each eye, then use the tip of the liner or round brush to place a dot of Titanium White on top of each blue dash for the sparkle, allowing a bit of the blue to show on each side. Use the liner brush and thinned Medium Brown Mix to paint a line of reflected color underneath each eye. If the eyes become too wide, simply go back and fill them in with the round brush and Ivory Black to make them narrower.

NOSE HIGHLIGHT: To paint the shine on the nose, use the flat side of the #6 sable brush to undercoat the area with a straight horizontal line of Medium Blue Mix (this line should not go clear across the nose). Rinse the paint out of the brush and pick up Titanium White, then paint a shorter horizontal line to highlight the center of the blue line. With a dry sable brush,

(Continued on Page 20)

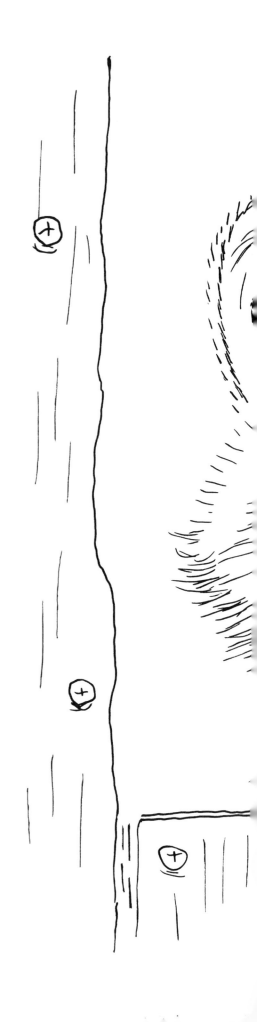

Curious Critter Magazine Rack

Front Panel Motif

Curious Critter
Magazine Rack

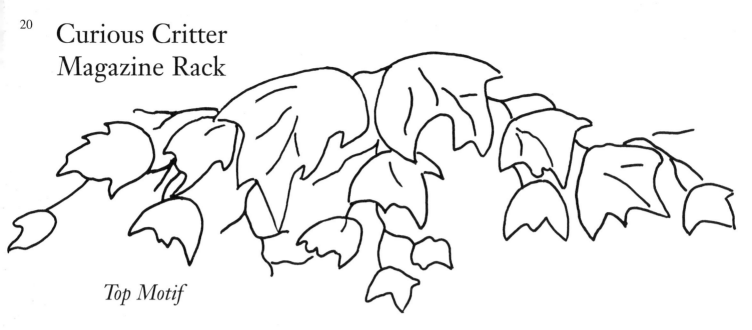

Top Motif

CURIOUS CRITTER MAGAZINE RACK
(Continued from Page 18)

soften this ever so slightly by pat blending the edges of the white. Because you are painting wet-on-wet, these colors will blend somewhat as they are applied, so you may need to repeat these steps until the desired shine is achieved. Always allow the paint to tack up before each additional application.

BARN BOARDS

With enough Liquin in the #10 flat bristle brush to thin the paint slightly, base the boards with Burnt Umber and Burnt Sienna, stroking vertically. These colors do not need to be mixed, rather picked up and applied randomly. You want the boards to look rustic and old, not newly painted. Referring to the color photo, you will notice spaces and grooves in the boards that have not been painted. Simply go around these areas, allowing the black basecoat to show through. Using the chisel edge of the #6 flat sable brush and the Medium Brown Mix, paint the ledges of the short boards, then paint a vertical line along the right edge of the tall board and the right edge of the short board on the far left. Highlight these same areas in the same manner, using the same brush and the Highlight White Mix. Put this highlight on heavier than you would a basecoat, and make the lines somewhat jagged.

Base the screw heads with the Medium Blue Mix and the #2 sable brush. After doing this, pick up a touch of Ivory Black on the corner of the brush and very lightly touch the screw heads here and there to dirty them up a bit. For more interest, I highlighted (using the same method) with a touch of Titanium White. Don't do this on every screw or in the exact same location. These should look smudged—you want the screw heads to look old, not shiny and new. Paint the shadows underneath the screw heads with Ivory Black and the round brush, then pat blend lightly to blur out the edges slightly. If desired, this shadow can be glazed in when the painting is completely dry. (Refer to "Glazing" under "General Terms and Techniques" in the front of the book.) I tend to think glazing adds a more realistic look to shading; but you may do whatever you find easier for you.

Now you should be ready to add the highlights and final detail work to the barn boards. You'll need to load the brush with a fair amount of paint and apply strokes vertically. With a #6 flat sable, streak the boards with all the various color mixes used for painting the raccoon. (I tend to do this with many of my paintings, using color to create overall balance.) Start by using the blue and brown mixes; add touches of Burnt Sienna here and there; then use the Highlight White Mix. The tall board (left side) should be the lightest of all. For the final detail work, use the liner brush and touches of both Burnt Umber and Ivory Black (thinned to ink consistency) to add some narrow crack lines. Toward the left side of each board, stroke touches of the Medium Blue Mix here and there to indicate reflected color. Use the Highlight White Mix to add a touch of reflected color to the ledge of the first short board on the left side.

BACKGROUND DETAIL

Using a dry bristle brush, scuff a bit of the Medium Blue Mix onto the black background around the raccoon, then add a touch of Titanium White to the dirty brush and lightly highlight the scuffed areas to the right of the raccoon. Gently pat blend these areas with a dry sable brush to soften them into the background.

DEVELOPING FUR

We are now ready to paint the fur. It is vital, at this point, to refer to the color photo often. Study the photo and pay close attention to the direction the hair strokes are going. Carefully review the "Layering Individual Hair Strokes" under "Developing Fur" in the front of the book. For the most part, we will be using the dagger brush for this work.

Starting at the top of the head, stroke individual hairs between the ears, using the Medium Blue Mix. Over these strokes, add lighter hairs with the Medium Brown Mix and the Highlight White Mix. Still using the dagger brush, add markings to the black part of the mask (around the eyes) with the Medium Blue Mix. If this appears to be too blue, add a bit of Ivory Black; if it looks too dark against the black, add a touch of Titanium White. Soften these markings with a dry sable brush. Using the #6 sable brush, pat the Medium Brown Mix on the muzzle, next to the nose. Paint the individual hairs above the nose, using the liner brush and Medium Brown Mix,

(Continued on Page 22)

Curious Critter
Magazine Rack
Pages 17-20 & 22

Resting Wolf
Pages 22-23 & 25-27

CURIOUS CRITTER MAGAZINE RACK
(Continued from Page 20)

Burnt Umber and Ivory Black separately. Shade the area between the mouth and nose with Ivory Black hair strokes (this shading will become a grayish color as you stroke into the white base color). Use the flat sable and Titanium White to paint the hair along the bottom edge of the mouth.

The fur on the body is painted with the same colors and mixes that were used for the head. Refer to the color photo to see where these colors are used. Make sure you take your time and work the fur in groupings. The area below the mouth is slightly shadowed, so paint fewer hairs and allow the black basecoat color to provide the shading.

To paint the hair in the white areas, dampen the 1/8" dagger brush (do not load with paint) and begin by pulling out individual hairs from the wet base color. Add a few hairs using touches of the Blue and Brown Mixes—mix a bit of Titanium White with these colors, as you do not want stark contrasts. Rinse the paint from the dagger brush, then pull the wet black paint from the dark areas around the eyes into the white patches of the forehead to make the edge of this area jagged. With the #0 liner, stroke the long hairs inside the ears, using Titanium White and Medium Brown Mix (thinned to ink consistency and applied separately). I also added some reflected color near the base of each ear and along the outer edges by painting a few hairs with the Medium Blue Mix. Next, thin Titanium White and pull out some whiskers.

LEAVES
Load the #6 flat sable with either Sap Green or Viridian, then tone it down by adding Burnt Sienna until you have a green you like. Use this color to base the leaves. Add Titanium White to the dirty brush and highlight some of the edges. Feel free at this point to add Burnt Sienna and Yellow Ochre if you want the leaves to show a bit of fall colors. If desired, add a touch of blue for reflected light. Paint branches with the #0 liner brush and the Medium Brown Mix. Paint veins, if desired, using the liner brush and the green basecoat color thinned to ink consistency. If the green is not dark enough to show up against the basecoat color, add Ivory Black.

GLAZING
When your painting is completely dry, glaze a bit of green (use a touch of either Sap Green or Viridian straight from the tube) here and there on the barn boards—this will tie everything together. Glazes need to be transparent, so do not add white to the greens. Follow the glazing instructions in the front of the book.

FINISHING
Allow a few days for the painting to dry, and then apply a light coat of Liquin to the design area. After the paint has had time to cure, protect the surface with the varnish of your choice.

Name this critter and you are finished!

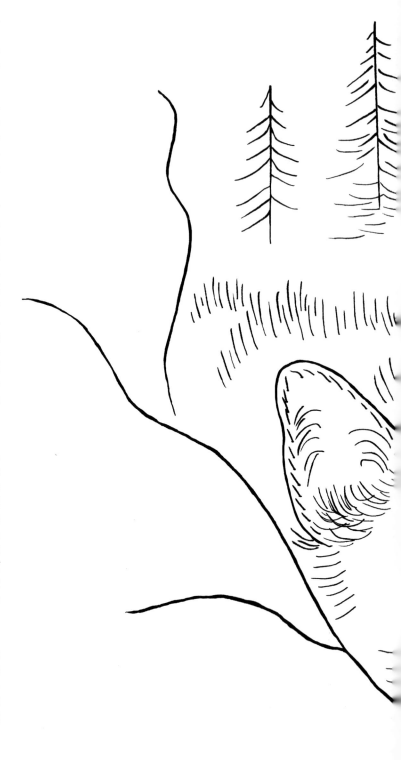

Resting Wolf

Instructions on Pages 25-27

H Barb
Halvorson
© 2001

Plaque Motif

*Enlarge pattern to fit
your vest*

EYES

RESTING WOLF

EAGLE

ROOSTER

RESTING WOLF
Nose and Mouth

BEAR CABINET
Nose and Mouth

Paw

Claws

LAYERING INDIVIDUAL HAIR STROKES

Hairs painted with a liner

Hairs painted with a dagger *(Bear Cabinet)*

Wrong way

Right way

Long hair painted with a fan brush *("Alone" Grey Wolf)*

GLAZING
Add shadows and highlights. After painting has dried, step can be repeated several times.

FENCE

Halvorson © 2001

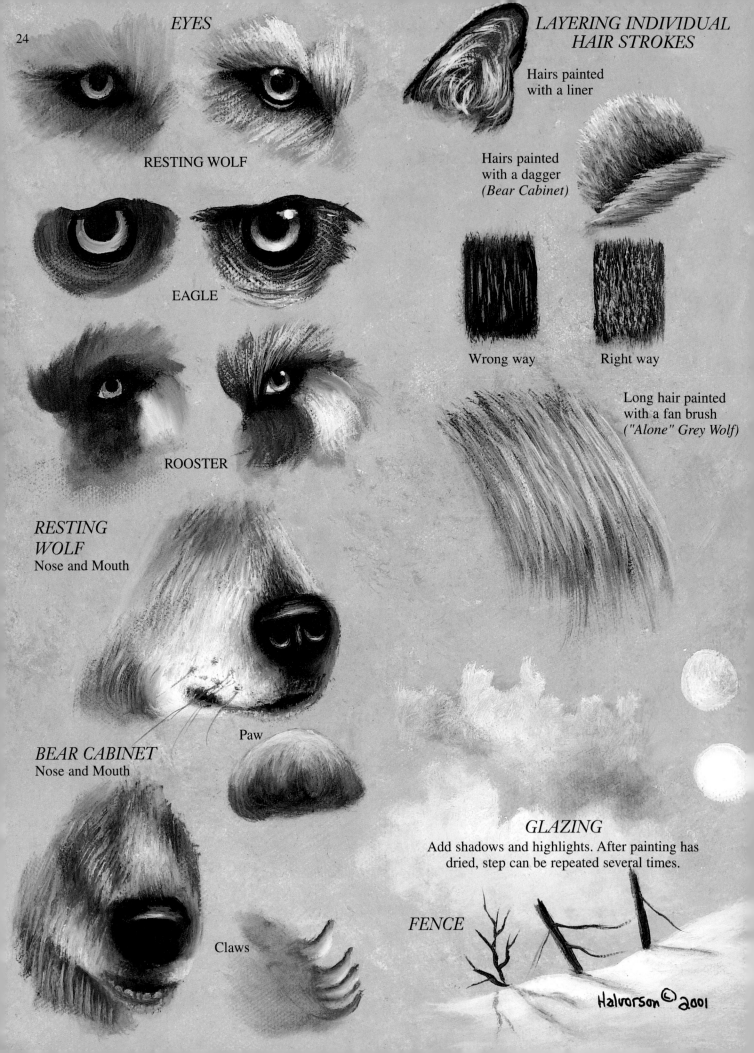

Resting Wolf
Oval Walnut Plaque and Vest
Color Photo on Page 21

PALETTE
WINSOR & NEWTON GRIFFIN ALKYD COLOURS
Burnt Sienna
Burnt Umber
French Ultramarine
Ivory Black
Sap Green (plaque)
Titanium White
Viridian (plaque)
Yellow Ochre

BRUSHES
Comb: 1/4"
Dagger: 1/8" (optional)
Fan: #2
Flat bristle: #6, #10
Flat sable: #2, #6
Round: #2
Script liner: #0

SPECIAL SUPPLIES
Black acrylic paint
Denim vest
Wood slice, walnut 11" x 14"

Plaque

PREPARATION
Follow the instructions under "Surface Preparation" in the "General Instructions" section of the book. (I did seal the walnut slice.) Basecoat the design area with two coats of black acrylic paint, leaving a band of natural wood showing around the edge. Let this dry, and transfer your pattern.

PAINTING INSTRUCTIONS
Please refer to "Developing Fur" at the front of the book. Also refer to the color worksheets when painting trees and wolf's eyes.

SKY AND DISTANT TREES
Load the #10 flat bristle brush with equal amounts of French Ultramarine and Ivory Black (very little paint on the brush) and loosely base the sky area just above the pine trees, stroking from side to side.

(Continued on Page 26)

Developing Fur

Base in colors, stroke in the direction the fur naturally grows. Do not apply paint heavily.

Start layering fur using either a dagger or comb brush. Watch the direction in which the fur is laying. Begin placing highlights on the eyes and nose.

Reinforce shadows, highlights and markings. Add accent color. Soften harsh edges. Glaze if necessary.

Halvorson
2001

RESTING WOLF

(Continued from Page 25)

To create the suggestion of distant pine trees across the top of the sky area, load one corner of a fan brush with the sky colors + a touch of Titanium White and pull the trunk lines. Form some of the trees by lightly tapping color on, moving up and then down the trunks. To set the trees in, pat across the bottoms with a dry, flat brush. After painting the more distinct pine trees just above the wolf's head (see instructions below), paint the suggestion of smaller trees to the right of the wolf's head, in the same manner as above.

PINE TREES

I mixed a variety of greens, using Sap Green, Viridian and French Ultramarine. If these colors seem too bright, tone down with Ivory Black or lighten with Titanium White. Use a liner or the chisel edge of a flat sable brush to pull the trunks. Load a corner of the fan brush, turn it over so the paint is on top of the brush, and then form the shape of each pine tree by tapping the color on, moving the brush from side to side. The highlights on the trees under the moon were tapped on with Titanium White.

WOLF

EYES: Using the #2 flat sable brush, base the lower half of the iris with Yellow Ochre and the upper corners with Burnt Sienna. Wipe the paint from the brush and gently pat where the two colors meet, to softly blend one into the other. Wash the paint from the brush, and fill in the pupil and the area around each eye with Ivory Black. Soften very slightly where the iris and the pupil meet. Looking carefully at the worksheet and color photo, notice the faint eyelash just above the sparkle in each eye, and the fine highlight line under each iris. Using the script liner and paint thinned to ink consistency, paint the eyelash with Burnt Sienna + Titanium White and paint the highlight line with Titanium White. Next, the sparkle is painted using either the liner or round brush. First paint a dash of Ivory Black + Titanium White; then place a dot of Titanium White on top of this. These eyes are not very big, nor very detailed; therefore, do not spend lots of time on them.

WHITE PATCHES AROUND EYES: Using a #6 flat sable brush, base these areas in with Titanium White + hints of Burnt Sienna and Yellow Ochre. After the paint has tacked up, use either the dagger or liner brush to pull individual hair strokes of Titanium White out from the edges of these patches and to pull Ivory Black strokes from the surrounding areas into the edges.

BODY AND HEAD: You will need both sable and bristle brushes for these areas—use the sable brushes where you want applications or blending to be soft and smooth. Before you paint these areas, study the color photo and worksheet very carefully and read through the painting instructions. Using a #6 flat bristle brush, base in the light and dark areas of the head and body (do not apply paint heavily). The dark areas of the body and the upper half of the head (including inside ears) are warm black, mixed with Ivory Black + a touch of Burnt Sienna. Base the white areas of the muzzle and the face with Titanium White. Use a clean brush to blend colors a bit where these areas touch. Shade under the nose with Ivory Black. Base the paw, nose and mouth with Ivory Black (try to paint around the pattern lines for the nostrils, mouth and paw; you will need to see these lines when you add highlights). Just above the nose, blend in a touch of Burnt Umber. Add the remaining patches of brownish color on the muzzle and body with mixes of Burnt Sienna, Yellow Ochre and Titanium White. When the paint on the paw area has tacked up, highlight with Titanium White + a little Burnt Umber, then soften the highlight by lightly patting it with a flat sable brush.

FINISHING THE NOSE: When painting the highlights on the nose, follow the pattern lines carefully. This is very important because, if the facial features are not placed and painted correctly, the entire face will look distorted. When the base layer of paint has tacked up, use Titanium White + a touch of Ivory Black to highlight the top of the nose, outline the bottom edges of the nostrils and paint the division between the nostrils. Soften the edges of the highlighted areas with a flat sable brush.

LAYERING INDIVIDUAL HAIRS: After the based areas have tacked up, start making individual hairs with a comb brush. I used almost all the colors in my palette (except greens), mixing a variety of grays, browns and blues. Using all these colors will tie everything together and provide balance. Thin your paint slightly with Liquin (paint *must not* be thick). For the first layers of hair, use colors that contrast with the base colors (lighter hairs over dark colors, and darker hairs over light colors), and remember to allow the base colors to show through for shading. I do this step several times, allowing each layer of hair to tack up before applying the next. The more layers you apply, the more realistic your fur will look. Toward the front of the face, use a liner or a round brush to paint shorter hairs. Make sure none of the hairs are too long, too straight or appear to be in a line. The fur toward the back appears to be in folds; soften where these folds meet the background. Hairs inside the ears are painted with a liner or a round brush and Titanium White. The bases of the whiskers are Ivory Black dots, applied with the tip of the liner or round brush. Make sure they are not very distinct. Soften the dots by gently patting them with a dry flat brush. If necessary, apply additional layers of hair to strengthen colors to make this wolf pretty. It will begin to come alive. Use a flat sable brush to soften and blur the very back section of the wolf. This will give the painting depth by making the front of the wolf appear to come forward. After painting the rocks, paint the whiskers with the liner brush and thinned Ivory Black.

ROCKS

Base the rocks in with Burnt Umber, using a #6 flat brush. Highlight the tops and sides with Burnt Sienna + Yellow Ochre + a touch of Titanium White. After the paint has tacked up slightly, lightly dampen the flat sable brush with Liquin and then use the chisel edge to softly brush some of the greens used for the trees onto the rocks to reflect these colors.

MOON

With a #2 flat sable brush, add a touch of Yellow Ochre to the Titanium White and base in the moon (keep the moon small). Using the flat sable slightly dampened with Liquin, pick up a blue color from the palette and pull a cloud over the moon.

GLAZING AND FINAL DETAIL

Study your painting (and refer to the color photos and worksheets) to decide whether there is a need to add or strengthen colors, etc. (shadows, highlights, fur markings, reflected color, additional hair). Review "Glazing and Final Detail" at the front of the book and follow instructions for applications. Sign your name and you are finished!

FINISHING

Allow the painting to dry again, then apply a thin coat of Liquin to the design area. When the paint has cured, varnish the surface with the product of your choice.

Vest

The "Resting Wolf" design on the denim vest was painted using the same alkyd colors used for the walnut slice. Lots and lots of compliments have come my way on this project. Before painting, launder the vest to remove sizing, but avoid using fabric softener when rinsing. For those of you who prefer to use fabric paint, just convert the colors—it would be very easy to do. When completely dry, heat set the paint by covering the design area with a dish towel or soft cloth and then pressing with a hot iron (be sure to keep the iron moving as you press). You will enjoy the end results, and you can even wear it, too!

You will notice that there is less detail on this wolf than on the wood slice painting. The reflected color on the rocks in this painting is French Ultramarine + Ivory Black + enough Titanium White to produce a blue-gray color.

Pattern on Pages 22-23

Early Winter

Color Photo on Page 28

This photo was taken in Missouri, on my way to a painting class. The Canada geese in the front were photographed at our own Lake Winona.

PALETTE
WINSOR & NEWTON GRIFFIN ALKYD COLOURS
Burnt Sienna
Burnt Umber
Cadmium Orange
Cadmium Red Light
Cadmium Yellow Light
Cerulean Blue Hue
French Ultramarine
Ivory Black
Titanium White
Yellow Ochre

BLUE MIX: Mix equal amounts of French Ultramarine and Ivory Black, and then add Titanium White until you have a medium blue color.

BRUSHES
Fan: #4
Flat bristle: #6, #10, #20
Flat sable: #2, #6
Round: #2
Script liner: #0

SPECIAL SUPPLIES
10" saw blade (or surface of your choice)
Gesso
Metal primer, gray

PREPARATION
Follow directions for metal preparation in the "General Instructions" section of the book. Transfer all of the design except the geese. When the painting is dry to the touch (this should take about a day, but may take a bit longer under warm, humid conditions), transfer the Canada geese pattern.

PAINTING INSTRUCTIONS
SKY
To create the varying colors and values in the sky, apply the paint by moving the brush in a circular motion, pulling one color into another. Using the #20 flat bristle brush and the Blue Mix + Ivory Black, begin by painting the darkest areas of the sky (above the roofline of the barn and above the foliage). Extend the color slightly below the foliage pattern lines. Pull this color upward (refer to color photo for color placement), picking up more and more Titanium White to make the sky ever lighter toward the top. Wash and blot the brush, then pick up Titanium White and touches of Cadmium Red Light, Cadmium Orange and Cadmium Yellow Light (each color is applied separately). Be careful not to use too much yellow or it will turn the sky green. Apply the tints along the top edge of the blade, blending down into the blue area.

When the sky has tacked up a bit, add some puffy clouds, using slightly heavier Titanium White (not much Liquin in the brush). To do this, load one corner of the #10 flat bristle brush, then turn it over so the paint is on the top of the brush. Form the clouds by "pushing" the paint onto the surface, leaving the heaviest deposit along the top edges of the clouds. To set the clouds in and soften the bottom edges, pull some of the wet sky color up into the white and then lightly blend. When painting cloud shapes, remember not to make them all the same size or lined up in a row. If you were to do this, the painting would lack depth.

BACKGROUND FOLIAGE AND TREE BRANCH
First, carefully study the background and pine tree illustrations on the color worksheet. Load a corner of the #4 fan brush with Burnt Sienna. With a tapping motion, apply the first layer of color for the bushes behind both sides of the barn. When doing this, be careful that the bushes are not all the same height or look like they are lined up in a row. For the next layer on the bushes, load the corner of the fan brush with

(Continued on Page 29)

Early Winter

Pages 27 & 29-31

Rooster

Pages 32-33

Kissin' Cowsins

Pages 34-36

EARLY WINTER
(Continued from Page 27)

various combinations of the following colors: Cadmium Red Light, Cadmium Orange and Cadmium Yellow Light. Apply these colors in clusters, rather than filling in a whole layer of the same color. You want the colors to get progressively lighter, ending with the lightest highlight color. Be careful not to cover the Burnt Sienna base color completely. The tree branch on the right side of the barn is stroked in using the #0 liner and thinned Burnt Umber. When this has tacked up slightly, add snow to the top or left side of the branches using Titanium White.

PINE TREES

Refer to the color worksheet for step-by-step illustrations. I painted the pine trees with a #6 flat bristle brush; however, if you prefer a smoother look, use a #6 flat sable. Load the brush with French Ultramarine + Cadmium Yellow Light (dark green—if too bright, tone it down with a touch of Burnt Sienna) and use the chisel edge to form the shape of the trees. Highlight the left side of each tree with Dirty White, then add a touch here and there to the right side as well. This will turn to a soft green.

BARN

SIDES: Load the #6 flat sable brush with Burnt Umber and Ivory Black, and then use the chisel edge to fill in under the roof edge on the lower left side of the barn. Start at the top and fill in about halfway down. Fill in the rest of the side with Burnt Sienna, beginning at the bottom and working up. Where the two colors meet, blend slightly. By using the chisel edge of the brush, you should start noticing just an indication of board lines—this side is almost a solid color. The upper left side, between the two roofs, is mostly Burnt Umber + Ivory Black; pick up a bit of Titanium White on the same dirty brush and lightly highlight the left side of this area. Paint the front of the barn the same way as the lower left side, but leave more space for highlight colors. The colors for the front area are various combinations of Cadmium Orange and Yellow Ochre added to Titanium White (refer to the color photo for placement). Later I added reflected color here and there, using a bit of the Blue Mix + a touch of Titanium White. Paint the horizontal supports and the trim around doors and windows with Ivory Black and the #0 liner. Add snow and highlights to these boards with Dirty White. Use the #6 flat sable with Burnt Umber + Ivory Black to fill in the large door and window openings, and where there are suggestions of broken boards. After the paint has tacked up, use Yellow Ochre + Titanium White to add extra highlights to the boards, and use Ivory Black to add extra shadows. Reinforce the shadow under the roof edge with Ivory Black. The cupola is simply Burnt Umber, highlighted on the right side with Titanium White + a touch of Yellow Ochre. Snow on cupola is Titanium White. The lightening rod is Burnt Umber.

ROOF: Both sections are painted the same. The center area is scuffed in using Burnt Umber and the #6 flat bristle brush. Be sure to apply strokes following the slant of the roofline. Fill in rest of the roof with the Blue Mix + Titanium White, then blend the colors together. Let the paint tack up a bit, and then use the #6 flat sable brush to add heavier applications of Titanium White to the lighter areas. Add a bit of Yellow Ochre to the brush and apply here and there to brighten the roof sections. I used a touch of Cerulean Blue Hue + Titanium White to accent here and there. This also adds contrast. Dampen the #0 liner brush with turpentine and pull down the white paint along the edges of the roof and cupola to create icicles. Make sure you pull these straight down, and not all the same length. Paint the boards inside the dark door (center of barn) with Dirty White; paint reflected color on the boards with the Blue Mix.

SNOW ON GROUND

With a #10 flat bristle brush and the Blue Mix + a touch of Ivory Black, paint the darkest shadowed areas of the snow. Wipe the brush and pick up Titanium White + Cerulean Blue Hue for the lighter shadows. Next, add the patches of white snow with Titanium White. (These areas will be glazed later.) Use some of the lighter sky colors to brighten the area in front of the right side of the barn and the area behind where the geese will be painted. To create shadows in front of the geese, darken the area with Ivory Black. Blend where the colors meet. Let this area dry completely, then use gray transfer paper to transfer the pattern for the geese.

FENCE

To paint the fence, use the #0 liner brush and thinned Ivory Black. Use Titanium White to add snow to the posts and rails.

CANADA GEESE

Refer to the color photo when painting the geese. Using a #2 flat sable brush, block in the light and dark areas: heads, necks and tail feathers are Ivory Black; breasts, shoulders and undersides are Titanium White, shaded with the Blue Mix + Ivory Black + a little Burnt Umber; remaining areas are filled in with Burnt Umber. To indicate feathers, add Titanium White to the Burnt Umber, and stroke in color using either the liner or a #2 round brush. Paint the shadows underneath the geese with Ivory Black + Blue Mix.

FRONT FOLIAGE

Paint the front foliage in the same way as the background foliage, using the same brushes and colors. Pull up weeds with a #0 liner brush, using basically all the colors in your palette. (Remember to thin the paint to ink consistency.) While you have the liner brush loaded with thinned paint in your hand, how about adding a few birds to the sky!

GLAZING

Allow the painting to dry thoroughly, then glaze the snow with touches of Yellow Ochre + Burnt Sienna. If desired, glaze to reinforce the shadows under the geese with Ivory Black + Blue Mix.

FINISHING

Allow the painting to dry completely, and apply a thin coat of Liquin. Allow the surface to dry again. To spatter the design with flecks of "snow," begin by thinning Titanium White with turpentine (on the palette). Next, stroke the corner of the #4 fan brush through the thinned paint, and practice spattering (move to a surface away from the painting) to test the paint consistency and size of the flecks. Holding the brush about a foot above the surface, spatter the flecks by pulling your forefinger across the bristles. If necessary, adjust the

(Continued on Page 30)

EARLY WINTER

(Continued from Page 29)

paint consistency by adding more paint or turpentine; adjust the size of the flecks by moving closer to or further away from the surface. When you are satisfied with the practicing results, cover any areas of the design where flecks are not desired, and spatter the design. If you are not happy with the results, wipe the flecks off and apply again. Sign your name, you are finished! When the spattering has dried completely, apply another thin coat of Liquin to the entire design. Allow time for the paint to cure, then varnish with the product of your choice.

Early Winter

Barb
Halvorson
© 2001

Rooster

Color Photo on Page 28

This fellow was photographed at a Wisconsin County Fair. Actually he was in a cage. (He likes it better where he is now—in a painting.) He's fun and easy to paint!

PALETTE
WINSOR & NEWTON GRIFFIN ALKYD COLOURS
Alizarin Crimson
Burnt Sienna
Cadmium Orange
Cadmium Red Light
Cadmium Yellow Light
French Ultramarine
Ivory Black
Sap Green
Titanium White
Yellow Ochre

BRUSHES
Fan: #2
Flat bristle: #6, #10
Flat sable: #6
Script liner: #0

SPECIAL SUPPLIES
Gesso
Metal primer
Old hand saw

PREPARATION
Follow the directions for metal preparation in the "General Instructions" section of the book. Transfer the pattern. Try free-handing the background bushes and trees; this will be good experience for you. Before doing this, study the color worksheets carefully.

PAINTING INSTRUCTIONS
SKY
Load a #10 flat bristle brush with equal amounts of Titanium White + French Ultramarine. Tone this color down with a touch of Ivory Black to create a medium blue. Base the sky area, stroking side to side. Wash the paint from the brush and dry it well with a paper towel. Now load one corner of the brush fairly heavily with Titanium White and tap in some clouds. (When forming clouds, remember that they should not be placed in a line or painted all the same size.) When there is no more paint in the brush, set the clouds in by gently patting along the very bottom of each one. This sky is in a very small area and there is not much detail, so there is no need to spend lots of time on it.

BACKGROUND TREES AND BUSHES
Again, begin by studying the color worksheet. Paint the bushes and trees starting with the most distant and working toward the rooster. When loading the fan brush, make sure you pick up a fairly heavy amount of paint and that it is evenly distributed on the brush; then, turn the brush over so the paint is on top when applying to the surface.

To paint the most distant trees, add touch of Ivory Black to the sky mixture (a shade darker than the sky color) and tap them in using the corner of the #2 fan brush. The darker tree foliage is applied the same way. Again, the load of paint needs to be fairly heavy. I used Sap Green and toned it down with Ivory Black. For a bluer green, add a touch of French Ultramarine. To lighten the mixes, add Cadmium Yellow Light and Titanium White.

Using the same colors and brush used for the tree foliage, paint bushes by tapping horizontally with the corner of the brush. Form the background bushes into clusters or groupings. If your bushes start looking like "arch" shapes, you are using too much of the fan brush—remember to use only the corner.

Pull out some tree branches with Ivory Black + Burnt Sienna. If you choose, add a highlight to the top of the branches with Titanium White + a touch of Yellow Ochre. Tap foliage here and there on the branches with Sap Green + a touch of Ivory Black.

Paint the pine trees with Sap Green + Ivory Black. Use a liner or the chisel edge of the #2 flat bristle brush to pull a line for the trunks. Using a corner of either the fan or flat bristle brush, form the trees by tapping up and down the trunk.

Using the same method as for the background bushes, tap in fall foliage with Burnt Sienna and highlight with both Cadmium Orange and Cadmium Yellow Light.

ROOSTER
COMB, WATTLE AND AREA AROUND EYE: Base these areas with Cadmium Red Light, using the #6 flat sable brush. Wipe the paint out of the brush with a paper towel, then load with Alizarin Crimson + Ivory Black to shade these areas. Soften where the two colors meet, using a dry flat sable brush. Load the flat sable brush with Cadmium Red Light + a touch of Titanium White, and highlight the wattle and the top of the comb (refer to the color photo for placement), using the chisel edge of the brush. Use the flat sable and Titanium White to paint the white patch on the cheek and to lightly stroke a highlight on the waddle, just below the patch. Pick up French Ultramarine + Titanium White to add reflected color to the front edges of the comb and wattle, then stroke a dab of this color over the upper right corner of the white patch on the cheek. After painting the feathers, you may need to come back and clean up the lower edges of the wattle, using the appropriate colors. If you prefer, you may paint the feathers first, then paint the wattle.

EYE: The eye is painted with the #0 liner brush. Base the iris with Yellow Ochre, and shade the corners with Burnt Sienna. Softly blend the colors together where they meet. Highlight the bottom of the iris with Cadmium Yellow Light. Paint the pupil with Ivory Black. The white in the corner of the eye is Titanium White. Using the tip of the liner brush, place a highlight dot of Titanium White on the pupil, at the one o'clock position.

HEAD, BEAK AND BODY: Use the #6 sable brush to roughly base these areas (do not fill in solidly) with Burnt Sienna + French Ultramarine (a brownish color). Using Burnt Sienna and stroking with the chisel edge of the flat sable brush, pull some streaks over the brownish color to represent feathers. Highlight on top of these colors with chisel strokes of Yellow Ochre + Titanium White. Use the same color mix to highlight the beak. For the detailed feathers on top of the head, use the #0 liner and the highlight mix thinned to ink consistency. With this color still in the brush, pull some thin strokes through the red area in front of the eye, then stroke through the yellow area just above the beak to add a bit of red.

GRASS AND WEEDS

Paint these with the same colors used for the pine trees and the foliage. Using the #0 liner, brush mix a lighter green to pull up individual weeds on the left side of the rooster. Using the darker mixes, pull some heavier strokes in front and along the right side of the rooster, then use the tip of the liner to tap the seed heads along each side of these grasses.

FINISHING

Sign your name! When completely dry, use the product of your choice to apply a protective finish to the design, following manufacturer's instructions.

Rooster

Halvorson © 2001

Kissin' Cowsins
Color Photo on Page 28

These cute cows were photographed on a farm in the small town of Ettrick, Wisconsin. I had pulled off the road to take a picture, when the owners drove by. They wondered what I was up to. Guess not many people stop and take pictures of their cows. This is one of my favorite photos. (I am also learning to enjoy the art of photography.)

My very good friend, who is also a painter, informed me that cows' hair is very short; so I did repaint these cows, just for her. But she is right, so watch that the hairs do not become too long. Mine could have been even a little shorter.

I want to dedicate this project to all the farmers out there. And also to the best farmer friend anyone could ever have. I really mean that! Sandy, this is for you!

PALETTE
WINSOR & NEWTON GRIFFIN ALKYD COLOURS
Burnt Sienna
Burnt Umber
Cadmium Red Light
Cadmium Yellow Light
Cerulean Blue Hue
French Ultramarine
Ivory Black
Sap Green
Titanium White
Yellow Ochre

BLUE MIX: Mix French Ultramarine and Ivory Black together, then add Titanium White until you have a medium gray-blue. You will be using this color in the sky and for the highlights on the cows.

BRUSHES
Comb: 1/4" (optional)
Dagger: 1/8"
Flat bristle: #6, #10, #20
Flat sable: #2, #6
Round: #2
Script liner: #0

SPECIAL SUPPLIES
Black acrylic paint, flat finish
Gesso
Masking tape
Metal primer

PREPARATION
Refer to "Surface Preparation" in the "General Instructions" section of the book and follow directions for preparing metal. Place masking tape along the top, bottom and side edges of the design area (from the center of one handle to the center of the other) so this area will remain white. Basecoat the rest of the can with black acrylic paint (I also basecoated the inside of the neck), and allow it to dry. Transfer the pattern.

PAINTING INSTRUCTIONS
SKY
Load the #20 flat bristle brush with the Blue Mix, and start filling in the top of the sky (the section between the neck and body of the can), beginning on the left side and working toward the right, stroking horizontally. As you paint, remember to leave some space open for the clouds. When you reach the middle of this area, add a touch of Ivory Black to the brush to create a darker gray-blue, and continue stroking toward the right side. By the time you reach the right side, you should have covered the top half of the sky. Wipe the brush on a paper towel. Using the same dirty brush, start adding Cerulean Blue Hue and Titanium White as you paint toward the lower portion of the sky area, again leaving openings for the clouds. As you get closer to the pattern lines for the cows, you may want to switch to the #6 flat bristle brush. Finish basing the sky area with various blues, including the Blue Mix. To paint the clouds, load the right corner of a dry #10 flat bristle brush with heavier Titanium White. Start forming the shapes by pushing the brush along the surface to deposit a more-textured application. Blend out the bottoms of the clouds by stroking horizontally with a #6 flat sable brush.

GRASS AREA
The area along the bottom of the design (behind where you see the tall grasses in the color photo) is loosely based in with Ivory Black + Sap Green. Start with a #10 flat bristle brush, and as you paint around the cows, switch to a #6 flat sable. Try to paint around pattern lines for the cows; if they get covered, just transfer the pattern lines again when the green is dry. Individual grass blades will be put in after the cows have been completed, during the finishing step.

COWS
I used mostly bristle brushes to paint the cows. Where I have used other types, they are specified in the instructions. Select brushes that are suitable for the size of the area being painted and for the desired texture you wish to achieve. Study the color photo and follow the color placement closely, and pay attention to the direction of the hair growth.

BROWN COW: With a #6 flat bristle brush, start blocking in the cow with three different color values. Scuff the paint in

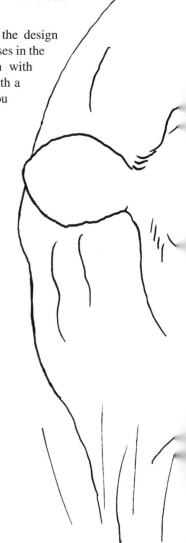

with short strokes, using Burnt Umber for the darkest value, Burnt Sienna for the middle value, and Titanium White + Yellow Ochre for the lightest value. Pat blend to soften these areas where they meet. While you're waiting for these areas to tack up, base in the eyes, nose and mouth area with a #2 flat sable brush and Ivory Black.

Start painting the individual hair (not too long—remember, cow hair is short!). Use either a #0 liner or a 1/8" dagger brush (most of the time, I switched back and forth between the two) and all the base color values to paint the hair. The lightest hair

along the top edge of the back is Cadmium Yellow Light + Titanium White. Add lighter hairs around the edge of the left ear with Titanium White. With Cadmium Red Light + Titanium White + a touch of Burnt Sienna, scuff color inside the ears and along the top of the mouth. Paint the textured white patches on the forehead, neck and belly with Titanium White. Paint the yellow textured patches above the nose, on the right ear and below the left ear with Yellow Ochre + Titanium White.

(Continued on Page 36)

Kissin' Cowsins

Halvorson © 2001

KISSIN' COWSINS
(Continued from Page 35)

When the eyes and nose are completely dry, use the #2 round brush to paint the sparkles in the eyes, placing a dash of Dirty White in the left eye only, and then a dot of Titanium White in each eye. The whites of the eyes are Dirty White, also painted with the #2 round. Highlight around the nostril and eyes with Blue Mix + Titanium White + a touch of Ivory Black (a darker medium gray-blue), using a very dry #2 round brush. Use the liner and a medium-gray mix of Titanium White + Ivory Black to paint the eyelashes on the right eye. Paint the white strokes above and below the eyes, and the patches around the nose and mouth with a heavier (more textured) coverage of Titanium White. Also add reflected color here and there, using the Blue Mix.

BLACK COW: With a flat #6 bristle brush and Ivory Black, scuff color on the entire cow, except for the white spots (don't forget to leave the pattern lines exposed). Load the #2 round brush with Burnt Sienna and Titanium White, and paint the lines above and below the eyes. At this point, stop and wait for the paint to dry completely. Using the #2 round, highlight each eye with a dash of Blue Mix; then add the sparkle dots and pull the very faint, thin line under each eyeball with Dirty White. Using the Blue Mix and the round brush, highlight around the nostrils and along the left side of the muzzle. Using a dry #6 bristle brush and the Blue Mix + a touch of Titanium White, scuff all the remaining highlights on the face, ears and body. Reinforce the highlight above the nostrils with Titanium White. Soften the edges of all these areas. Paint the white spots with Titanium White. Scuff a little Ivory Black into the spots to dirty them up a bit, and then soften around the outer edges of the spots. Using either the dagger or liner, pull the hair over the forehead and along the outer edge of left ear with Ivory Black. Pull some very fine individual hairs along edge of right ear, using the small dagger or comb and Titanium White. Referring to the instructions for the brown cow, scuff color along top of mouth.

GRASSES ALONG BOTTOM OF DESIGN

Using the #0 liner brush and a variety of green mixes, paint the grasses. Remember to thin the paint to ink consistency. Start by mixing a dark green with Ivory Black + Sap Green, then add both Titanium White and Cadmium Yellow Light, in varying amounts, to create lighter and warmer shades. If desired, you could even add reflected color, using a bit of the Blue Mix here and there.

GLAZING

Allow the entire painting to dry completely, then review the glazing instructions in the "General Terms and Techniques" section of the book. Using a flat sable brush and Burnt Umber, glaze over the darkest areas of the brown cow. You may want to add a touch of Ivory Black when glazing the left side of the belly (in the "V" shape just under the neck). Glaze Ivory Black over all black areas of the black cow (do not glaze over the highlighted areas) and over grasses under the right side of the black cow to add contrast. You are finished! Sign your name!

FINISHING

When the glazed areas have dried thoroughly, apply a thin coat of Liquin to the entire design area. Allow time for the paint to cure, then apply the varnish of your choice.

Four Seasons

Color Photo on Back Cover

Every fall season, my husband and I pick up freshly fallen autumn leaves. Last year I painted the leaves, then we matted and framed them for craft shows. They were really a big hit. When collecting leaves for this project, make sure the leaves are not brittle or dried out. These mini paintings could also be painted on four small canvases and framed. Because the scenes are small and quite simple, I have included individual instructions for each season. The leaves are quite fragile, so very soft brushes are required.

PALETTE
WINSOR & NEWTON GRIFFIN ALKYD COLOURS
Alizarin Crimson
Burnt Sienna
Burnt Umber
Cadmium Orange
Cadmium Yellow Light
Cerulean Blue Hue
French Ultramarine
Ivory Black
Sap Green
Titanium White
Yellow Ochre

BRUSHES
Flat sables: #2, #6
Round: #2
Script liner: #0

Leaves

SPECIAL SUPPLIES
Color-fast paper (for mounting leaves)
Frame with glass
Glycerin (We buy the bigger bottle of glycerin, ordered through a pharmacy.)
Laminate roller (optional)
Real leaves
Spray adhesive

PREPARATION

Soak the leaves in glycerin (I use a small square, flat-bottomed plastic tub for soaking) just until they are thoroughly wet all over. Press the leaves between layers of paper toweling, cover toweling and leaves with a flat book or board and place a rock or other heavy object on top. Allow the leaves to dry completely (this could take several months; read manufacturer's suggestions on glycerin container). When dry, transfer pattern (I used Saral transfer paper).

PAINTING INSTRUCTIONS
SPRING SCENE

(Refer to the color worksheet for an illustration of the shed.) To paint the tree and bushes behind the shed, load one corner of the #6 flat sable brush, and form shapes by tapping the colors in. Trees and bushes to the left of the shed are Sap Green; bushes to the right are Alizarin Crimson. Tap in highlights on the bushes to the right with Titanium White, forming groups and clusters. This will avoid the look of having placed dots here and there.

Next, start painting the shed. Block in the upper half of the left side with Burnt Umber. Pick up Burnt Sienna + a touch of Titanium White and block in the rest of this side, starting at the bottom and working upward. Blend where the two colors meet, using vertical strokes. Use the chisel edge of the brush to pull streaks of Burnt Umber down into the bottom section—this will indicate board lines. Do the front side the same way, but use Burnt Sienna to block in the top section, and Yellow Ochre + Titanium White to block in the bottom section, then blend where the colors meet. Make sure there is enough contrast between the two sides of the building. Scuff the roof in, using various mixes of the colors used on the sides. Use the #0 liner and both Burnt Umber and Burnt Sienna (thinned to ink consistency) to add some board lines to the roof. Shade under the edges of the roof and add the detail lines to the front sections with Burnt Umber + a touch of Ivory Black. Use a clean liner to highlight the roof edges with Yellow Ochre + Titanium White.

Add another colorful bush behind the foreground tree, following the instructions for the bushes to the right of the shed. Base the trunk and heavy branches of the large tree with Ivory Black + a touch of Burnt Umber; paint the ends of the branches with thinned Burnt Umber. Paint the grass area between the shed and large tree with Sap Green; use the flat side of the #6 sable brush to pull short, downward strokes. Tap highlights with Titanium White + Yellow Ochre. Highlight the left side of the tree, using the chisel edge of the #2 flat sable and French Ultramarine + Ivory Black + Titanium White, then

Four Seasons

Spring Motif

Halvorson 2001

use Titanium White for a few bright highlights. Fill in the foreground grass area, again basing with Sap Green and highlighting with Titanium White + Yellow Ochre. Add a touch of Ivory Black to Sap Green, and shade the grass area around the tree. Sign your name!

FALL SCENE

The sky behind the barn is painted with various shades of purple using combinations of French Ultramarine, Alizarin Crimson, and Titanium White. Apply colors using a #6 flat sable brush, stroking horizontally. Use the corner of the same brush to pat in the fall foliage. Colors are combinations of Burnt Sienna and small amounts of Alizarin Crimson. Highlights are applied in groups or clusters, using Cadmium Yellow Light and Cadmium Orange. Use the chisel edge of the #2 flat sable to begin shaping the pine trees to the left of the barn. Keep the tops thinner, the bottoms wider. Highlight the left side of each tree with Cadmium Yellow Light + Titanium White.

Scuff in the top of silo and the dark area on the right side of the barn with Burnt Umber. Base the remaining sides of the barn with Burnt Sienna, and highlight with Yellow Ochre + Titanium White. Base the barn roof and silo with Yellow Ochre + Titanium White. Shade under the edges of the roof and paint the door opening with Burnt Umber. Paint the lines on the roof with thinned Burnt Umber. Using thinned Ivory Black on the #0 liner, outline the edges of the roof, the top of the silo and around the door to define these areas; then paint the lines on the body of the silo, and paint in the windows. Highlight above the roof edges with Titanium White. The trim on the windows and across the top of the door, and the upper back corner of the roof are French Ultramarine + Titanium White.

Paint the grass around the front of the barn with Yellow Ochre + Titanium White. The path is painted with side-to-side strokes of Burnt Umber, using the #2 sable (keep the path

Fall Motif

Halvorson 2001

(Continued on Page 38)

FOUR SEASONS

(Continued from Page 37)

small). Paint the rest of the grass area with Yellow Ochre + Burnt Sienna. Add a touch of Burnt Umber to the darker areas of the grass. Using the #2 round brush, paint the post with Ivory Black, and highlight the left side with Titanium White + a touch of French Ultramarine. You are finished!

WINTER SCENE

Begin with the distant background pine trees. Use the chisel edge of the #2 flat sable brush to paint the basic tree shapes (refer to worksheet illustration) with French Ultramarine + Ivory Black + a hint of Titanium White. With this color still in the brush, pick up only enough Titanium White to mix a medium blue, and then highlight these shapes, mostly on the left sides. Now paint the hill of snow behind the barn. The shadowed area is painted with Ivory Black + French Ultramarine + Titanium White. Start at the bottom of the hill with the darkest value, and as you paint upward, pick up more and more Titanium White. By the time you reach the top of the hill, the color on the brush should be almost all white with just a touch of blue. Using a dry brush, blend where the light and dark areas meet, stroking side to side.

Use the chisel edge of the #2 flat sable brush and Sap Green + Ivory Black to paint the pine trees at the base of the hill. Highlight the lighter trees with Titanium White. Use the colors used to paint the background pine trees to add a few bushes next to the left side of the barn.

Still using the #2 flat sable, apply Burnt Umber shading under the eaves of the barn. Using the same brush, base the rest of the siding and the door on the left side with Alizarin Crimson + Yellow Ochre (a rustic red color). Using the chisel edge of the brush, pull streaks from the shading color, down through the red areas. Block in the left side of the barn roof with Titanium White + a hints of French Ultramarine and Ivory Black. Wipe the brush. Pick up a touch of French Ultramarine + Ivory Black and block in the right side, then blend the areas together. If the blue seems too bright, add a

Winter Motif

Halvorson©2001

touch more Ivory Black. The left side of the stone foundation (shaded side) is based in with Burnt Umber, the right side with Burnt Sienna. Add detail, and dot in the stone shapes, using a #2 round brush and Dirty White. Paint door on right side and both windows with a liner brush and Burnt Umber + Ivory Black. Paint the silo and the small building with Titanium White. On the dirty brush, pick up a touch of Cerulean Blue Hue + a hint of Ivory Black and shade the right side and roof of silo, and the right side of the building. Pick up a bit more Ivory Black on the dirty brush and shade the bottom of the silo, under the edges of the roof of the building, and paint the windows and the door. Use the liner brush and Ivory Black + Titanium White to paint the detail lines below the silo roof. Using the #0 liner, pick up heavier Titanium White (not thinned) and pull icicles from the edges of the roofs of the barn and small building. Snow around the barn is scuffed in, using the same colors used to paint the hill. Add a touch of Cerulean Blue Hue here and there in the snow. "'Tis the Season"… Winter is finished!

Four Seasons

Summer Motif

Halvorson © 2001

SUMMER SCENE

Background foliage is painted with French Ultramarine toned down with Ivory Black. Apply using the chisel edge of the #6 sable brush, stroking up and down. Tap in the highlights with Titanium White. Using the liner brush, thin Burnt Umber to ink consistency and paint the branches of the tree behind the barn. Add leaves by tapping in Sap Green with a #2 round brush. Even though this is a small area, try to paint the leaves in clusters. Highlight some of the leaf foliage with Titanium White + a touch of Cadmium Yellow Light.

Paint the barn in the same way as the Fall Scene design, using the same brushes and colors. I added a little more reflected blue to the front and roof of this building. The right side of the barn is almost solid Ivory Black + a touch of Burnt Umber.

Along the edges of the path, lay in a tiny bit of Burnt Umber; then loosely pull this in toward the center just a bit, using the chisel edge of the brush. Make sure the path strokes are all horizontal and parallel. Clean the brush and lay in various combinations of Burnt Sienna, Yellow Ochre and Titanium White up the path. With a #6 flat sable brush and Sap Green + a touch of Titanium White, apply very short up-and-down strokes to paint the grass. Shaded areas are Sap Green + Ivory Black. For the lighter areas, clean the brush and load with Titanium White + a touch of Yellow Ochre.

FINISHING

Allow the paint to dry completely. I mounted these leaves on a light-fast, charcoal-color paper that was purchased from a craft store. I'm sure there are other papers that would work just as well. You may also want to consider matting the paper. Decide in advance exactly how you want to arrange the leaves on the paper. Spray the back of each leaf with craft adhesive and allow the glue to tack up; then, when ready, carefully place the leaves on the paper. I then used a rubber laminate roller (the type used for laminating counter tops) to smooth the leaves once they were set in place. Allow a few days for the glue to dry, then frame the leaves behind glass.

Chicken Feeder

This is an extra pattern for you to try on your own. I paint the feeders often for craft shows. Painting instructions are about the same as for the Fall Scene in the "Leaves" project—see what you can do. The feeders can also be used to hold potpourri or candy.

SPECIAL SUPPLIES

Chicken feeder (found in most hardware stores)
Gesso, optional

PREPARATION

Since it can be somewhat difficult to paint on glass using oil or alkyd paints (paint moves and does not cover too well, some people prefer to cover the entire design area with two coats of gesso before painting the design. However, I chose to paint right on the glass. Transfer or freehand the design.

PAINTING INSTRUCTIONS

Although I used all the same colors as used for the Fall Scene painting, I didn't always paint each object or area in exactly the same way. And I added elements that were not in the original design. Be creative and experiment with colors, and refer to the other projects for painting ideas and instructions.

Basically I begin by basing the main areas, making sure the paint covers the surface. You will still see through the paint, and it will not look too good at this point, but do not spend much time on this step. I add no detail yet. I allow the paint to dry for about 6 hours, and then paint the main areas again (even a third time, if necessary). I then add the detail work. When the grass was dry, I freehanded the chickens. They are little smudges of Titanium White, shaded with Ivory Black or French Ultramarine Blue. The red areas on tops of the heads are Alizarin Crimson, highlighted with Cadmium Red Light or Cadmium Orange. The beaks and legs are Yellow Ochre.

FINISHING

Protect the surface with the varnish of your choice. For added decoration, tie a bow to the base of the feeder.

(Continued on Page 40)

Chicken Feeder

Halvorson
© 2001

FOUR SEASONS
(Continued from Page 39)
Wood Box

This is another extra project for you to experiment with on your own. Notice something familiar about this painting? I took the barn from the winter scene and the big tree from the spring scene. I took the fence posts and path from the fall and summer scenes. Do your own thing! See what you can come up with.

SPECIAL SUPPLIES
Gesso
Wood stain (I used golden oak.)

PREPARATION
Refer to "Surface Preparation" in the front of the book. Apply gesso to the design surface. Stain the rest of the box. When dry, transfer the design.

PAINTING INSTRUCTIONS
Refer to other projects, photos and color worksheets for ideas on how to paint the different elements. Don't be afraid to experiment with color choices of your own. I added straw (Yellow Ochre) in the loft window of this barn.

GLAZING
If necessary, add glazes when the painting is completely dry.

FINISHING
Apply a coat of Liquin to the entire design when the glazes have dried. Varnish when the paint has had time to cure.

Four Seasons
Wood Box

© Halvorson 2001

"Alone" Grey Wolf
Color Photo on Page 45

After painting and studying wolves for the past few years, the wolf has become one of my very favorite subjects to paint. This painting is not difficult, but requires patience…and lots of time. The individual hairs were painted with both sizes of the dagger brush, the fan brush and the liner brush. This painting is never truly finished. Even now, I continue to add hairs and highlights, and to deepen shadows by glazing. You are finished when you are satisfied. This wolf was photographed at Como Park Zoo in St. Paul, Minnesota.

PALETTE
WINSOR & NEWTON GRIFFIN ALKYD COLOURS
Burnt Sienna
Burnt Umber
Cadmium Orange
Cerulean Blue Hue
Ivory Black
Titanium White
Yellow Ochre
WEBER PERMALBA OIL COLORS
Indanthrone Blue

BRUSHES
Dagger: 1/8", 3/8"
Fan: #4
Flat bristle: #10, #20
Flat sable: #6
Round: #2
Script liner: #0

SPECIAL SUPPLIES
16" x 20" stretched canvas

PREPARATION

No preparation is necessary for primed canvas. Transfer pattern.

PAINTING INSTRUCTIONS

Please refer to the color worksheets when painting the wolf and birch trees.

BACKGROUND AND DISTANT TREES

Fully load the #20 flat bristle brush with a mix of Indanthrone Blue and Ivory Black. This should be a very dark mix, almost black. Brushing side to side, paint the dark portion of the background, all the way across the canvas, with solid coverage. Soften any apparent brush marks by stroking back and forth (very gently) with a large clean bristle brush. As you soften the area around the wolf, allow the paint to drift slightly below the pattern lines, onto the wolf, but make sure the pattern lines are still visible. This will eliminate any white spacing around the wolf that might otherwise be visible after you have painted him.

Next, paint just an indication of the distant trees above and behind the wolf's head, using a color that is just a shade lighter in value than the background mix. If there is still a bit of the dark background mix in the brush, add a touch of Titanium White to it; or, if necessary, reload the brush by picking up a very small amount of the background mix + a touch of Titanium White. Then, very simply, stroke up and down each trunk to apply just enough color to define the shapes. Thoroughly wipe the paint from the brush with a paper towel; then using a very light touch, stroke across the trunks to soften the application. Remember, these are *distant* trees.

Wash and blot the brush, then use one corner to brush mix Cerulean Blue Hue + Titanium White + a touch of Ivory Black. Applying the paint in a circular motion, fill in the unpainted canvas area (the area around the wolf's face and the open space to the left of the foreground birch tree). This is the first step in creating a foggy look in this area.

BIRCH TREES (Basing)

With the #20 flat bristle brush, pick up Ivory Black and add small amounts of Titanium White until you have a medium gray color. Birch trees tend to have natural horizontal markings; therefore, your strokes must also be horizontal. Keeping the paint slightly thinned with Liquin will produce a smooth look. Base in the three trees behind the wolf and the large tree in the foreground. While you wait for the paint to tack up, move on to the wolf.

WOLF

Before painting the wolf, study the color photo carefully and read "Developing Fur" in the front of the book.

EYES: Study the color worksheet illustration carefully. These eyes are much the same as those in the "Resting Wolf" painting; please refer to that project for basic instructions and brush information. The right eye on this wolf has a very thin highlight line of Titanium White across the top, just under the white patch. For the shading across the very tops of the corners of the irises, use Burnt Umber. Pat blend where colors meet.

BASING IN (Body and Head): Base the entire wolf (except for the white patches around the eyes) with a #10 flat bristle brush, stroking in the direction the natural growth pattern of the hair. First, base in all the dark areas with Ivory Black + a touch of Burnt Sienna + a touch of Indanthrone Blue (very warm black). Start with the dark area inside each ear and the shadow behind the right ear. Continue down the head, then to the shadow underneath the neck and the dark area at the back portion of the wolf. Base the brown areas next to the black areas with Burnt Umber + Burnt Sienna mixed in equal parts. Base in all the light areas (except eye patches) with Titanium White. Base in the nose and mouth with Ivory Black, painting around the pattern lines (you will need the lines when highlighting). If you find the #10 flat bristle is too large for these areas, switch to a smaller flat brush. Using a #6 flat sable brush, base the white patches around the eyes areas with Titanium White.

DETAIL ON BIRCH TREES

All the birch trees will be painted in basically the same fashion. However, it will be necessary to refer to the color photo and worksheet illustrations for color placement. Notice that the dark and light colors are not in the same locations on all trees. Also notice that the large foreground tree to the left of the wolf's face is the closest and, therefore, the sharpest in contrast and lightest overall; and because the three trees on the right side are pushed further into the distance, they are a bit darker and slightly blurred. When painting the markings, shadows and highlights, make sure they don't end up looking like stripes around the tree: you don't want all the different colors to meet, or end, in the center of the tree. Load only one flat side of a slightly damp #10 flat bristle brush (paint should not be thinned), picking up enough paint to apply a heavier, more textured coverage. Using the chisel edge of the brush and stroking horizontally, apply Ivory Black to the dark side and pull color toward the opposite side. Next, add touches of Titanium White + a touch of Cerulean Blue Hue to the middle areas of the trees, and pull the color outward. Apply Titanium White + a touch of Yellow Ochre to the appropriate side of each tree and pull toward the opposite side. The lightest highlights are on the right side of the large foreground tree on the left. If desired, a stronger highlight could be added here and there on this tree, using just a touch of pure Titanium White straight from the tube. As a final step on the distant trees, use a clean, dry #20 flat bristle brush to very gently (barely touching!) stroke across each tree to blur them slightly.

LEAVES

The leaves are painted loosely and have little detail. Pick up very little Burnt Sienna on a #6 bristle brush and form the basic shapes of the leaves. When you run out of paint on the brush, gently pat the edges to soften and blur them. For the highlight areas, stroke on a touches of Yellow Ochre and Cadmium Orange mixed separately with Titanium White. Again, blur the edges of some leaves. Paint the stems with the #0 liner and thinned Burnt Umber + a touch of Ivory Black.

DEVELOPING FUR

This is when the time consuming part comes in. Before you begin, review the section "Layering Individual Hair Strokes" under "Developing Fur" in the front of the book. Refer back to these instructions and the color photo often. Remember to pay attention to the direction and length of the hairs. To paint the

(Continued on Page 44)

"Alone" Grey Wolf

Instructions on Pages 40-41 & 44

H Barb Halvorson © 2001

*Match and attach with the
pattern section on pages 46-47*

"ALONE" GREY WOLF
(Continued from Page 41)

individual hairs, use both sizes of the dagger brush, and use the #4 fan brush for the longer hairs toward the back.

By now you should have several colors on the palette paper, in a wide range of values. Use these colors to paint hair. Start by pulling fine hair lines out from the upper edges of the white eye patches (just turp on the tip of the brush); then clean the brush and pull in some black lines from the surrounding areas. Clean the brush again and stroke Burnt Sienna and Yellow Ochre into the patches.

In the black areas of the wolf, use variations of the lighter blues, browns and yellows from the palette; to the white areas, add variations of the darker shades and middle-value colors. If you study the color photo, you will see that all the areas show individual hairs of all these colors. Watch for contrast—do not let the wolf become all gray, all black or all white. If this starts to happen, come back to the general light and dark areas and add the colors that are missing. As you study the photo, notice that some areas of the brightest hair on the back are a yellowish color. For these areas, add a few strokes of Titanium White + Yellow Ochre. Using either the dagger or the #0 liner brush, paint the long hair inside the ear with Titanium White, and the very short, bright hair around the outer and lower edges of the ear with Yellow Ochre + Titanium White. Repeat these steps as often as necessary to finish layering hair. Remember, this process cannot be completed in one class setting. I warned you that this painting would be time consuming! But I think you will enjoy the end results.

MUZZLE DETAIL AND WHISKERS

With a #2 round brush, highlight the nose and the nostril with Ivory Black + a touch of Dirty White. This should be a dark gray color that barely shows and has very little detail. Soften with the #6 flat sable, barely touching the edges of the highlight. Referring to the photo, notice the shadow underneath and to the side of the nose. To apply this shading, you can either pull the Ivory Black from the nose, or pick up a very small amount of Ivory Black with a #6 sable brush. Blur this out slightly by gently patting the edges with a flat sable brush. Add the very short hairs above and below the mouth with a damp liner or dagger brush by pulling Titanium White down from the based area above the mouth, and using a touch of light blue for the hair strokes above the mouth. Paint the whiskers with the #0 liner and thinned Ivory Black, using the very tip of the brush to pull the thin lines. Practice this step on palette paper first—whiskers can be hard. It is easy to get them too thick; so the trick is to make sure the paint is very runny. With a dry #2 round brush, gently tap the bases of the whiskers to set them in.

FINAL DETAIL ON GROUND AREA

Using a dry #20 flat bristle brush (no Liquin on the brush), add a bit of Titanium White + a touch of Yellow Ochre to the lightest area of the painting (to the left of the wolf's face). Use only a corner of the brush to apply the paint, moving the bristles in a circular motion. Gently blend this color down into the blue and white area until you have no paint left in the brush. This should be very blurred. In exactly the same manner, use the darkest background mix to shade the area around the base of the large birch tree (left side of painting), and the area

to the right of the tree that is next to the wolf's chest. (If you do not have any of the background mix left on the palette, brush mix a small amount of Ivory Black + touches of Burnt Sienna and Indanthrone Blue.) Again, soften these applications into the light areas to blur them in.

BRANCHES

Before putting in the branches, make sure the paint on that area of the wolf is quite dry and that you are finished with this area. To base the branches, start with the #6 flat sable brush for the widest sections of the limbs, then switch to the #0 liner when you get to the thinner sections. Base the right sides of the branches with Burnt Umber + a touch of Ivory Black (thinned to ink consistency); base the left sides with Burnt Sienna + a touch of Titanium White. To add snow to the tops of the branches, load a clean #0 liner brush with Titanium White (not thinned) + just a hint of the blue background mix. Put this on rather thickly, placing it above the darker base color. For sharp highlights here and there, use Titanium White straight from the tube. Do not cover up all the snow with these highlights—you want to see some contrast.

GLAZING (Optional)

This is a fun painting for learning basic glazing techniques. First, allow the paint to dry completely; then read the glazing instructions in the "General Terms and Techniques" section at front of the book. Using the #6 flat sable, apply a thin layer of Liquin over the distant (very dark) background trees. Pick up Ivory Black + a touch of Indanthrone Blue, then stroke color into the layer of Liquin to deepen the color of the trees. If you wish, use this same glaze to darken the wolf's eyes and deepen the shadows underneath the nose and neck—or wherever you would like to establish more contrast. If you want to reflect a bit more sunlight on the brightest hairs, use thin glazes of Yellow Ochre or Cadmium Orange. Be sure to test these colors on a small area first. What happens if you mess up???? Simply wipe the glaze off with a soft paper towel—but don't wait too long! Sign your name and be proud of your painting! You did it!

FINISHING

When the paint has dried thoroughly, apply a layer of Liquin to the entire painting. Allow time for curing, and varnish with the product of your choice.

Patterns on Pages
42-43 & 46-47